The
TAROT
of the
MAGI

D1447172

the TAROT of the MAGI

by Carlyle A. Pushong

A Newcastle Classic

Newcastle Publishing
North Hollywood, California

ISBN: 0-87877-192-1
A Newcastle Book
First printing 1994
10 9 8 7 6 5 4 3 2 1
Printed in the United States of America.

Originally published in 1967 by Regency Press, London, England

Cover design © 1994 Michele Lanci-Altomare

This book has been written for
NANETTE MARIE
as a very small appreciation
of her outstanding courage

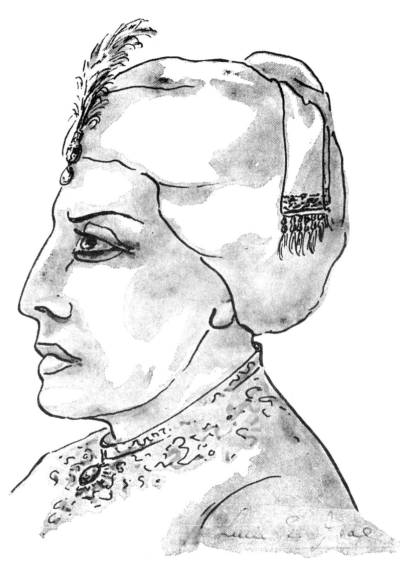

An Indian Prince, one of the writer's Spirit Guides
who assists him in all matters of the mind

CONTENTS

PREFACE

With the growing interest in the Tarot, this book which sets out to elucidate the most ancient and accurate of divinatory systems is a Must. Here we have no woolly abstractions, or pseudo-Kabalistic mumbo-jumbo which unfortunately forms the basis of the majority of books on the Tarot.

I have known CARLYLE PUSHONG for many years, and have often been amazed by his scholarship, occult knowledge, and rare qualities of mind. He indicates with great clarity the Paths to Glory that the earnest seeker of the Truth may well wish to follow in his pursuit of the Godhead that exists within each one of us. From this one gathers that the divinatory aspect of the Tarot is but its lesser masque.

In this age of national and international disharmony, it is my considered opinion that this concise dissertation on the Tarot, will go a long way towards removing the smog of misanthropy that clouds human affairs, and is a progressive step towards the Brotherhood of Man.

"To please one feeling heart, for one calm, thoughtful hour,
Go, little book! content if thine the power."

(*E. Jesse*)

Sd. DR. DOUGLAS M. BAKER,
B.A., M.R.C.S., L.R.C.P.
LONDON

INTRODUCTION

A symbol is an abstract representation of a reality, a representation which the human intelligence accepts and possibly theorises about, but cannot entirely grasp its fundamental aspect. In an age when computers have been enslaved to do much of man's thinking, the human computer Man, tends to become atrophied at the level of his ultra-consciousness where he could easily outrival any mechanical computer and thereby uncover some of the secrets of the profound structure of the Universe. A symbol, however, is not a diagrammatic outline of reality and signifies nothing to the mass of mankind. It requires a flash of illumination, Ultra-consciousness, or the Awareness of mysticism, for man to communicate his findings at an intelligible level, always assuming that the discovery is to the good of mankind.

A symbol is a masque except to the illuminated Adept who in a state of Awareness interprets and understands the non-dimensional aspect of what he sees with the inward eye. It would be arrogance of the worst kind to consider that Man holds the key to unlock every mystery of the Universe, but he does contain within himself those dormant forces which in a state of Awareness can be roused to activity for the betterment of humanity at large. The Ultra-conscious man will be the Superman of the Aquarian Age, for the Aquarian Age is witnessing a return to the age of the Adept. "Nothing in the world can resist the cumulative ardour of a sufficiently large number of enlightened minds working together in organized groups." (Teilhard de Chardin.) To the Adept past, present, and future ARE, for it is only our consciousness that moves. The mystic seeks freedom to BECOME in the midst of an eternity which IS, for this is the way in which human destiny is tied to the whole Universe: this indeed is the aim of theoretical physics today.

Linked to Ultra-consciousness is the phenomenon of Synchronism, namely, the inter-connexion between events which apparently have no cause for relationship, but may yet serve as significant catalysts on the human level. The observation of such coincidences may lead to discoveries so far reaching in their consequences as to almost belong to the realm of science-fiction in terms of "fantastic reality".

The new Superman of the Aquarian Age is already in our midst, but he is unlikely to be betrayed either by his fellows or by mutants of the Piscean Age who are still Earth Travellers.

In the short outline of the Tarot which follows, I have attempted to present this wonderful occult system divorced from the sometimes abstract meanderings of acknowledged authorities on the subject, who in the main attempt to correlate the Tarot so closely with the Kabala, that I am sure that our non-existent entity the "average man", ends up in a virtual state of mental confusion. I believe that the Tarot stands or falls by its own merits. Admittedly the Tarot does correlate with the Kabala at certain points, but this correlation is also patently evident with other metaphysical systems, with none so strongly as with Sankara's Vedanta. To this end, I have added an Appendix which deals with Sankara's doctrine of Maya. The metaphysical concept of Maya is difficult to put into language and I have done the best I could within my limitations.

In my treatment of the Tarot with particular reference to the twenty-two cards of the Major Arcana or Mysteries, it will doubtlessly be said by some that much of what I have stated is "old hat". To such critics all I can say in reply is that—"there is nothing new, except what has been forgotten." (Mlle. Bertin.)

I have not attempted a history of the origin and development of the Tarot, but have made passing historical references of this order, throughout the text. The specific Tarot which is illustrated and under reference is the famous Marseille Tarot pack.

Lastly, I do not lay claim to any superior inspiration in producing this short outline of the wonderful Tarot. On the other hand, the key word behind my labours has been "TRY". If anything, I consider this book as a Primer for anyone seeking to gain some fundamental knowledge of the Tarot with a view to proceeding to more advanced research. Apart from this, there is no message!

> "Have you not heard his silent steps?
> He comes, comes, ever comes.
> Every moment and every age, every day
> and every night he comes, comes, ever comes."

> ("*Gitanjali*"—*Rabindranath Tagore*)

The Tarot of the Magi

CHAPTER I

ARCANUM ZERO: THE FOOL

THE FOOL

Concurrent with the dawn of human consciousness, myths and symbols began to take their place as the Algebra of Wisdom in a form readily acceptable and digested by the ever growing human mind. Whereas myths transmitted ideas to man's emotional centres, symbols conveyed ideas to his ever formative mind. Down the corridors of time, symbols though they have changed their shapes ever and anon, have however perennially retained the same meanings, portraying as always, universal and transcendental truths, the intensity of vision varying with the inward eye of the Watcher on the Shore. The symbology of the Tarot is no less, which in its fullest interpretation tears the veil from Isis and leaves her naked in her loveliness. The Tarot is the key to life the great adventure and is in point of fact the Way of Life on earth en route to the Life Eternal.

The Fool is the un-numbered card (which has the cipher zero) of the Tarot Major Arcana. In the Marseille pack the card is called "Le Mat", to wit, the Motley Fool, a throwback to the Medieval Court Jester who was often "A wise fool amongst the foolish wise." In this card we see a man in motley clothes who appears to be walking quite unaware of his danger to the edge of a precipice with his head turned aside. Over his right shoulder he carries a small bundle on a stick, the totality of his Karmic experiences which he will take with him into the next world or his future incarnation. The Fool also seems unaware of the dog pawing him from behind, the dog that is the evolved descendant of wolves, but now man's best animal friend who glories in the happiness of his God, represented by man. A crocodile is often portrayed (in other packs) in the waters below, ready to receive Le Mat when he steps off from the precipice: the crocodile to the ancient Egyptians symbolised deity. The overall message would appear to be that—Through folly men shall learn wisdom, for those who do not make mistakes never make anything.

Much profound poppycock has been written about this un-numbered card—"The Fool", and many alleged authorities tend to give its esoteric and mundane interpretation after expatiating on Arcana I to XXI. However, with my Sagittarian élan and with no intention of hubris, I am dealing with this card first. Le Mat links with Arcanum XVII—"The Star", and is the bridge of Hope between manifestation and the for ever manifest, and is symbolic of both states. Apropos of bridges, the Fool also represents the foolish Adept pursuing the path of self destruction, of no-return, when giving into some malign temptation, his Folly rather than Fate ruins what might have been: the Pons Asinorum of Occult-ism. This then is the great magical side-track between the grade of Adept Minor and that of Magus, when the Adept-student ceases to be a Magician and becomes a Fool. In the highest sense of the card the Fool represents the accomplished Adept.

Man is the hub of the wheel around which the rest of creation revolves. Whilst the power of the Magus in Arcanum I is potential, is limited in the extent and range of its application, and merely points in the direction of a yet uncertain Path, the Fool in the purest sense of the card sees the Reality behind Reality, and sees the illusory nature of Past, Present and Future as Maya, one indivisible illusion. The Fool therefore does not represent one of the Tarot Paths, but is the starting point from which the twenty-one Tarot Paths should be pursued, commencing with the Magus, Arcanum I, where the Will of the Seeker is as yet not conceived and lacks direction.

A zero symbolically represents Super-consciousness.

"Earth bears no balsam for mistakes;
Men crown the Knave and scourge the tool
That did his will; but Thou, O God,
Be merciful to me, a fool!"

(*The Fool's Prayer—E. R. Sill*)

CHAPTER II

ARCANUM I: THE JUGGLER

I

THE JUGGLER

Arcanum I is the Magus, commonly known as "The Juggler", and in the Marseille Tarot as— "Le Bateleur", the Conjuror. A young man stands before a table wearing the hat of Hermes in the shape of the figure eight lying on its side: ∞ is also the symbol for Infinity. In the hand of his raised left arm (portraying the feminine aspect) pointing towards the heavens, is a Wand, the Caduceus of Hermes, which is channelling down the Astral Power via his Will. His right arm and hand (portraying the masculine aspect) in a reversed position is holding a wafer, orb, or perhaps a pentacle, for the precise detail is not clear.

The symbology would appear to be the flow of the divine power and revelation, attracted by the Caduceus of Hermes to the unconscious and as yet undirected Will of the Magus, uniting the Microcosm with the Macrocosm. On the table are a number of articles, some of which defy description, owing to bad copying or perhaps deliberate obscuration, but which are not germane to the esoteric interpretation of the card. Perhaps the articles on the table were originally meant to be the four symbols of the Minor Arcana, namely Sceptres or Wands, Cups, Swords and Pentacles.

The first move of the fledgling Seeker begins at Arcanum I calling into being the growth processes of Involution. The process of Evolution commences with Arcanum XI—"Strength" or "La Force", also called "The Enchantress": the Solar power of the Gnostic Lion. The close link between Arcanum I and XI is also clearly indicated, for these are the only two cards of the Major Arcana that have the Hat of Hermes as a form of head-dress. Card XI also marks the half-way ascent of the initiate in the Major Arcana. Whereas the cipher zero proper to "Le Mat" or "The Fool", cannot be defined or divided, the digit I of "The Magus" though it cannot be divided, can be defined. The number one on the Divine Plane signifies the first principle and unity, it is the divine sign of universal life, it is the number of the Divine Being in every religion. On the Occult Plane the number one represents the soul of nature, the soul of the elements, and the active causative and creative forces of the unseen universe. On the Material Plane one stands for the effort of Will on the part of an individual.

Miracles in the relative sense are anything beyond the level of our mental understanding. "The Magus" is the link between God and Nature operating on the three planes of man, namely, the Mental, Astral, and Physical, for the purpose of establishing unity in diversity, by means of a Faith bolstered by knowledge, to wit, "Magic" or Melchizedek. The Tarot premises that every man is his own magician. The aims of the Magus which belong to the physical plane can be brought to fruition by the concentration of the imagination and Will on the desired object/objective, thereby effecting a transition from the plastic astral plane, to the third dimensional physical plane.

> "A mighty purpose rises large and slow
> From out the fluctuations of my soul,
> As, ghost-like from the dim and tumbling sea
> Starts the completed moon."
>
> (*Alexander Smith*)

CHAPTER III

ARCANUM II:
THE HIGH PRIESTESS

Arcanum II in the Marseille Tarot is entitled "La Papesse", a harkening back to the legendary female Pope of the Middle Ages, a legend with a less than minimal substratum of truth, although there was a surfeit of Popes unworthy of the name. The Marseille representation is certainly incomplete, and ought to show Isis or Artemis resplendent in her veil of Light seated between the two pillars of Solomon's temple, Jakin and Boaz. Jakin on her right representing the Sun and Boaz on her left representing the Moon: she in turn is Isis, veiled Priestess of the Silver Star, the Guardian at the Door of the Sanctuary, the equilibrating force, the Eternal She, the Spirit of the Mysteries, the link between the Above and the Below. On her lap is a partly unrolled scroll of the

THE PRIESTESS

Tora, the Divine Law or the Book of Thoth, the Tetragrammaton, none other than the Universal Principle which manifests itself in every sphere of life. At the threshold of the mysteries are the pillars of Jakin and Boaz, representing good and evil, or more likely Karma and Dharma (Justice). On the head of the High Priestess is the horned orb, the cow being sacred to Isis. At the

20

feet of the High Priestess is a crescent Moon, and on her breast a Solar cross the sigil of the Moon, again indicative of her equilibrating function. Behind Isis enthroned, clothed in her garment of all suffusing light, is a backdrop or curtain screening the vistas of all that is transcendent.

In the effulgent Light of Isis, the Magus of Arcanum I seeks to strike a balance between what is earthwise transitory, and what is astralwise the eternal unmanifest. Having struck this balance, the Magus of the fifth Race acquires in some measure, that perception and unlimited sight which was the natural inheritance of the Atlantean Fourth Race of Men who perished some 11,000 years ago, and who walked the then known earth which stretched from the sources of the Oxus and Jaxartes in prehistoric India to the two Americas.

Less esoterically, the High Priestess in Arcanum II represents the female creative force, the Mother of Wisdom who rules all women, a triform goddess, personifying in turn—

1. Luna the consort of Sol.
2. Diana the celibate Huntress.
3. Hecate, the mistress of evil enchantments, the dark power of the Moon.

Two on the Divine Plane stands for the mother principle, the negative and feminine aspect of the Astral. On the Occult Plane two represents the more material soul of the earth, with the expression of unity through woman—$(1+1)$. On the Material Plane, two indicates a period when one is caught up in the Samsaric round becoming a creature of destiny.

"The sublimity of Wisdom is to do those things living, which are to be desired when dying."

(Jeremy Taylor)

CHAPTER IV

ARCANUM III: THE EMPRESS

III

Arcanum III of the Marseille Tarot is "L'Imperatrice" or the Empress, where the illustration of the Empress of Nature shows her enthroned, wearing a bejewelled crown. She holds a sceptre in her left hand, and held to her right side is a shield picturing an eagle sacred to Zeus. Sometimes in other Tarot packs the symbol of Venus — ♀ is shown on the shield. The Empress represents Mother Nature, the Earth Mother, the Empress of the Planet Earth, the female aspect of the Planetary Being, the great Unmanifest Feminine Principle, mindless, but absolutely good, pure and true, and in her highest aspects links with Ain Soph of the Kabala.

THE EMPRESS

God's creation on Earth is the Planetary Being, mindless, yet potentially God on Earth, the Zeitgeist of the World. Man in his evolutionary spiritual upsurge becomes increasingly aware of his responsibility towards others, there being ever present the attendant consequences of Karma and Dharma (Justice), if he oversteps real human values through either egoism or closes his senses to the "Voice of Conscience". Rapport with the Planetary Being cannot be established either on the plane of intellectuality or by thought-force extended as in prayer, but through the heart

22

of not only the Magus, but through the hearts of all mankind in a spirit of communion with God's legatee the Planetary Being, enriching It spiritually thereby, till eventually the kingdom of God reigns on Earth.

The Empress of Nature, the "Queen of Life" is less esoterically the human aspect of love, Venus on earth, a triune goddess in mythological symbology to be associated with:

(i) Astarte or Ashtaroth the Semetic goddess, expressing the procreative continuity of physical human love, for "Nothing is created, but everything is born."

(ii) Aphrodite, linking with human affinity between like minds conjoined by soul affinity, in which sex need play no part and in terms of relativity is permanent. The end product may well be works of Art.

(iii) Hermaphrodite, the synthesis of Wisdom and Understanding (c.f. Hermaphroditos, the son of Hermes and Aphrodite, who grew together with the nymph Salmacis into one person), Cosmic withal and comparable to the love between Guru* and Chela†.

The close correspondence between Arcanum III and Arcanum I and II, will now become more apparent, for the Magus—Arcanum I having penetrated the mysteries of Isis—Arcanum II, is now mellowed by the benign influence of the Earth Mother whose overshadowing love is both Universal and cosmic. Arcanum I, II, and III may be correlated with Truth, Wisdom and Love-understanding, respectively. Arcanum III (three being the number of movement) synonymous with the vivifying force Azoth, is the key which unlocks the door to Initiation. The number three on the Divine Plane signifies the universal vivifying force Azoth. On the Occult Plane three stands for the driving forces of energy (e.g. the Egyptian or far Eastern Lingam), which unites positive and negative, male and female. On the material Plane, three stands for the sexwise conjunction of male and female.

> "Nature's self, which is the breath of God,
> Or His pure word by miracle revealed."
>
> *(Wordsworth)*

* Sage & Preceptor
† Disciple

CHAPTER V

The Emperor, Arcanum IV, "L' Empereur" of the Marseille Tarot, shows an elderly crowned and long-bearded man seated on a throne, holding a sceptre in his right hand, at the top of which is a Hermetic Globe surmounted by a cross, indicating in a general way the ascendancy of the spiritual over the temporal, or of the Initiate over Matter. The Marseille illustration does vary in some other packs, in as much as the Emperor is shown seated on a cubic stone, but the overall and fundamental pictograph is as has been described. The Emperor is a Solar figure, the personification of the liberated man, identical with Light, Martian in quality and endowed with Wisdom. He is the active male counterpart fortified by the vivifying force of the Alchemical Azoth as distinct

THE EMPEROR

from his female aspect the Empress of Nature, Arcanum III, who reflects the passive light of the Moon. The Emperor represents the material world, government, and temporal power, which even though it might stem from Divine inspiration, is none the less spiritually extroverted, relative, and restricted in its range of application.

Here then is the Fourth Step in Initiation which premises

that no man can compromise with his conscience. The Emperor is therefore the Emperor of Wisdom, the occult instructed Emperor activated by Martian fire, the vital force of Kundalini, the Serpent-fire, equating with the Alchemical Azoth, as a prelude to Cosmic synthesis. The esoteric shibboleth of the Fourth Initiation or Great Arcanum is I.N.R.I. (Igne natura renovatur integra)—"All nature is regenerated by fire".

There are pitfalls on the way to the Fourth Initiation, all of which have their genesis in the all too common human weakness of Pride, which could show in any one or a combination of the following not very laudable foibles—Foolhardiness, Selfishness, Callousness, Susceptibility, Aggressiveness, and an unbridled passion to desire, posses, dominate or to be admired. The Book of Thoth will be seen to deal at all twenty-one stages on the paths to final Liberation, with the fundamental concept of birth often in the sense of new opportunity, and with its purpose Initiation, ranging from the aims of the Magus in Arcanum I to the end product, "The Universe", Arcanum XXI. The first four cards indicate this plan very clearly, for the Magus assisted by the Wisdom of Isis, and in communion with the female and male aspects of the Planetary Being, acquires control over Matter, as a foretaste of further spiritual progress, yet to come, for "the truth must be veiled, yet not hidden from the people." (Eliphas Levi.)

The number four on the Divine Plane signifies the universal creating fluid, the primordial substance which is the origin of all matter, Prakriti. On the Occult Plane four stands for the soul of the universe, the immortal constituent of all manifestation in the third dimension. Whilst on the Material Plane four signifies the end-product of previous action, or the termination of some matter in hand.

Tarot interpretation works on the premise that in nature there is no such thing as chance or accident. It would seem that the Tarot stimulates the powers of clairvoyance inherent in all men and with particular reference to the delineator, inducing a psychic or mental state favourable to divination, awakening in him images of his superconsciousness. This line of thought has been introduced now because it is hoped that at this stage the interest of the reader has been sufficiently aroused to reflect rather more deeply on what many people consider merely as a card game or just another form of divination. The symbols on the Tarot cards

of the Major Arcana have been identified with paintings found on
the four walls in ancient Egyptian temples, where the ancient
Egyptian priest-initiates tossed divining sticks upon an altar in
order to interpret whatever problem was at issue. The interpreta-
tions were based on the picture or pictures at which the sticks
pointed. Though the mnemonic Tarot symbols are stereotypes, they
are also timeless prototypes depicting perennial human traits
with an endless variety of mutations and flux in the life of Man
the Earth-traveller. "The Kingly Way" indeed, to man's eternal
quest to find a place in the Spiritual Sun.

THE EMPEROR

"Distinguish'd link in being's endless chain!
Midway from nothing to the Deity."

(*Dr. E. Young*)

CHAPTER VI

ARCANUM V:
THE GREAT HIEROPHANT

Arcanum V is the Great Hierophant, or "The Pope", in the
Marseille Tarot called "Le Pape".
The French title of "Le Pape"
leaves no doubt that this was in-
tentionally chosen for placating
the persecuting Papal hierarchy
of mediaeval times. The Papal
Tiara on the head of the seated
Pontiff was intended as a further
sop to the persecution of Rome in
a bid to make the Tarot cards
popular and suggestively inno-
cuous. Held in the left hand of
the Pontiff is a sceptre with a
triple cross, a symbol of his mas-
tery in the three worlds, the physical, the astral, and the mental.
His right hand is uplifted with
two fingers raised in benediction
over of the laity with their backs
turned, wearing strange circular
hats. A similar blue-hatted figure
is on the left hand side of the

THE HIEROPHANT

pictograph, and a third arm and hand comes into the illustration
from the right: for any arcane significance, these badly drawn
figures are void of meaning. The Pope in ecclesiastical attire is
seated on his throne which has two fluted uprights at its back
(c.f the throne of Isis, and the pillars of Jakin and Boaz in
Arcanum II), representing the duality of Law and Liberty, conjoined with Man's Free-Will to seek the path of his choice.

Without labouring the point, I would like to recapitulate
that a great fetish is made by Tarot experts to associate and

equate the Tarot Cards with particular reference to the Major
Arcana, as closely as possible with the Kabala. This association
is often so intricately woven that one loses sight of the Tarot
as such, which in the last analysis emerges as a by-product of
the Kabala. In this frame of reference, I humbly suggest that
there is an undoubted link, common denominator, or "what have
you", between all esoteric systems worthy of the name, but each
in turn rises or falls by its own merits. Passing references will
be made from time to time to the Kabala and also to other
Hermetic or Eastern esoteric systems, but these observations will
in the main be "en passant".

The Great Hierophant is the esoteric opposite of Isis (Arcanum II) the dispenser of Divine Wisdom. Although in the highest
sense, the Hierophant is above the affairs of this world, in terms
of practicality he represents the expression of the Creative Will.
He is a Solar sign dispensing practical and oral instruction in
contra-distinction to Isis, for he has no need of the scroll or Tora
of Isis since his teaching is exoteric. He obtains his wisdom from
Arcanum XIX "The Sun", is activated by Arcanum IV "The
Emperor", and is the manifest form of Arcanum III "The Empress
of Nature", the female aspect of the Planetary Being. The Great
Hierophant points the way to occult priesthood along the paths
of Silence and Watchfulness, and enables the Seeker to discover
the inherent potential power or ability which lies dormant within
each one of us, in order to make our lives actively creative. Herein
lies the occult secret of the astral power of the upright human
pentagram,* leading to the creation of the "idea-force", or even to

* *The Star of the Magi*
The upright pentagram, the Flaming Pentacle, the allegorical Star of the
Magi, represents man with his hands outstretched in blessing, his feet firmly
spread on the earth, and his head erect in the direction of the stars. In this
position man represents the White Magician who has activated the force of the
coiled serpent-Kundalini, at the base of the spine, and has by his will-power
subjugated all elemental forces.
The reversed pentagram employed by the Black Magician enables him
to harness the astral forces of evil to do his bidding with far reaching
diabolical results.
The number 5 standing midway in the decade (10), is the number of
man acting as God's legate in the Plan Divine, and is the most occultly
significant of all the digits.
Occultly added $5 = 1 + 2 + 3 + 4 + 5 = 15$, the number also of Trump XV
—The Devil. However, by occult reduction $15 = 1 + 5 = 6$, the number of
the Christ-force or the Divinity in man. Man represented by the number 5
stands at the cross-roads between the powers of good and evil.

the creation of the Plastic Mediator, the Magnum Opus of the Mage, but the Earth Traveller would do well to hasten slowly.

The number five on the Divine Plane stands for Universal life, law and intelligence. On the Occult Plane five signifies the power of faith over the human imagination, the faith to be creatively new. At a higher level five represents the faith that links with initiation. On the Material Plane five signifies animate life and intellect, and in general terms, Reunion.

"Let us be silent, that we may hear the whispers of the gods."
                                                (*Emerson*)

CHAPTER VII

ARCANUM VI: THE LOVERS

Arcanum VI, "L'Amoureux" of
the Marseille Tarot, is commonly
referred to as "The Lovers",
though the latter title is some-
what inapt owing to the difference in connotation of the word
"Love" as understood by Gaul
and Anglo-Saxon. It must be
clearly established at the outset,
that though Arcanum VI is difficult to interpret, it hardly represents the naive distinction between
good and evil which some experts
ask us to accept, for this is not
the primary purpose of the Tarot.
Duality of aspect in terms of good
and evil may possibly be implied,
but certainly not distinction between these two relative terms.

In the illustration we see
Eros or Hermes aiming his Karmic arrow at the central figure of
a group of three people. The central figure though in male attire,
does in appearance look androgynous, and facially and physically
seems to incorporate the essential characteristics of the two female
figures by whom he is flanked. The Eros of ancient Greek mythology was not the sexual Cupid of latter days, but was connected
with the world's creation. In the pictograph his divinely directed
Karmic arrow represents the Divine Will which will help in Man's
Regeneration through Transformation, and inevitably links with

Arcanum XIII, "The Reaper" or "Death". Man is continually at war with himself, in as much as his higher self, namely, the Soul, is in conflict with his lower self, namely, the spirit in its material body.

Eros, the son of Venus, is the discriminating and divinely directed Will, shooting a Karmic arrow of outrageous fortune at the dual man of Gemini. It was in the beginning when the "Lords of Flame" from Venus visited the earth, that hermaphrodite man was divided into the dual-sexed condition of male and female. That the androgyne births of the Third Root Race, will be repeated in the Sixth Root Race yet to come, is the esoteric message of Arcanum VI. Eros operates earth-wise on the Plane of Maya. Maya can only be ultimately destroyed when the Seeker of Truth perceives the Unity of the Creator, in which state of being the initiate becomes an Adept and Cosmic Consciousness is his to have and to hold, for he has attained liberation from the Samsaric round whilst still on earth, namely, Jivanmukti.

The number six on the Divine Plane signifies charity or Divine Love. On the Occult Plane "six" stands for equilibration, in terms of both attraction and repulsion, and represents the duality of every problem. On the Material Plane "six" may signify either good or evil, implying involvement, and union, sexual or otherwise.

> "From harmony, from heavenly harmony
> This universal Frame began:
> From harmony to harmony
> Through all the compass of the notes it ran,
> The diapason closing full in Man."

(A song for St. Cecelia's Day)

CHAPTER VIII

ARCANUM VII:
THE CHARIOT

Arcanum VII, The Chariot, "Le Chariot" of the Marseille Tarot shows a king in a chariot drawn by two horses, with a sceptre in his right hand. The king appears to be riding in triumph and apparently has full control over the horses which however are proceeding unguided, and in a docile manner. In some Tarot packs two lions or two oxen are yoked to the chariot, but horses would seem to be a better choice, for the horse as always is a Solar symbol. The "Chariot of the Sun" therefore promises the Magus occult help via the Lunar controls of manifest life. Negatively, the Full Moon can also be the great Illusion Bringer: the warning is abundantly clear. On either shoulder of the charioteer King is a face, each face looking in the opposite direction. Once again the

Samsaric warning of the attendant dangers of Maya are indicated, namely, the shadow should not be mistaken for the substance.

There could be an Arcane reference here to Elijah (Book of Kings) the prophet who was in communion with Jehovah on Mt. Carmel, during the prophet's struggle with Ahab and the priests of Baal. This Elijah, and the same Elias of the Transfiguration, who became the prototype of the "Wandering Jew", was in the time of Ahab whirled into heaven in a "Chariot of Fire". Without labouring the point, the undoubted reference to an U.F.O. is all too clear. The legend of the "Wandering Jew" has persisted down the ages and in many countries, and is older than Christianity or recorded history. From the Judaic Elijah we have the "Wandering Jew" and the herald of the Messiah. In moslem lore we have "Al-Khedr" (The Green), because Elijah is credited with the discovery of the River of Youth: he is also known as "Zerib bar Elia", namely, the prophet Elijah. The Christian version refers to the "Wandering Jew" who reviled Jesus on the way to His Crucifixion, as Ahasuerus (as to how this name was applied to the "Wandering Jew" baffles all understanding). He has even been equated with the Antichrist of the Second Coming. Folklore sometimes unhappily transmutes a saintly character into an ignoble one. Two basic themes emerge from these legends: the first is the curse of abnormal longevity on this earth, and secondly, the problem of guilt, repentance, and redemption.

The Kingly charioteer is undoubtedly the androgynous young man of Arcanum VI—"The Lovers", who is now moving ahead apparently in triumph but still beset by dangers in as much as he must control his carnal and spiritual urges, in order that he may face up to the responsibilities and trials that lie ahead. The pictograph shows four columns supporting the canopy of the chariot which links with the fourfold Hermetic maxim: "To Dare, to be Silent, to Know, and to Try". A firm correlation exists between Arcanum V—The Great Hierophant, and Arcanum VII—"Le Chariot". Whereas the Great Hierophant is exalted on the plane of Wisdom, the higher Self or the Kingly Charioteer, "trailing clouds of glory", operates on the plane of understanding at the physical level of Malkuth of the Kabala, heralding the onset of Awareness. Here we see the metaphysical equilibrating aspect of the Samsaric birth-death of the higher Self in the person of the Charioteer King in order to enable him to function on the physical plane by the horse the swiftest transportation of days past, a Solar symbol. The King of the Chariot has successfully harnessed his Divine and Human natures in order that he might set a seal on his spirituality, and thus in a sense has reached the end of his first stage on the road to Adeptship.

Number seven on the Divine Plane stands for the Fatherhood

c

of God and divine realisation; on the Mystic Plane for the Astral Light by means of which all thought forms are transmitted; and on the Material Plane, for victory gained after struggle. The number seven also governs the sea, sea commerce, and journeys on water; and is the number of the nomad.

"Hail to the Chief who in triumph advances!"

(Scott—Lady of the Lake)

CHAPTER IX

ARCANUM VIII:
THE BALANCE

"All crimes shall cease, and
   ancient fraud shall fail,
Returning Justice lift aloft her
   scale,
Peace o'er the world her olive
   wand extend,
And White-robed Innocence
   from heaven descend."

The above quatrain is from Pope's Christian hymn the "Messiah", expressing his poetic yearning for the return of the Golden Age of gods and goddesses, in this case for the return of the goddess Themis (Justice) who sat by the side of Jove, and was represented as holding aloft a pair of scales in which she weighed the claims of mortals. In Arcanum VIII — "The Balance", Themis of Greek mythology, or "La Justice" of the Marseille Tarot, a female figure is shown seated on a throne which has two sphere capped pillars. She wears a curious turban-like headdress with a double circle depicted on it, and surmounted by a crown. In her right hand she holds a double-edged sword pointing upwards, and in her left hand supports a pair of scales which forms a figure eight if viewed upon its side, and could read as the mathematical symbol for Infinity and therefore as the symbol for Life Eternal. The recurrence of the number two in the overall symbology indicates firstly, the unity of one plus one expressed through woman; and secondly, the duality or binary nature of all manifest existence or experiences and the necessity for their just equilibration. The upright sword represents the sword of discrimination, a double-edged weapon which can cut both ways, namely, Karma, for everything must be paid for either in this life or in the next.

The Divine Justice here under reference, is not blindfolded in the illustration of Arcanum VIII and is absolutely impartial in contradistinction to Human justice which is imperfect and to a variable extent blind. Arcanum VIII may also be said to represent self-initiation in life's "Siege Perilous", for when we look introspectively and without bias at our true self, the picture seen by the inward eye can be shamefully distressing.

Occult knowledge both theoretical and practical attained so far by the Kingly Charioteer of Arcanum VII is now confronted by the sword of Themis, for little Mercy can be expected by the false Magus who has abused his powers. Kabala-wise, the seated Themis represents Chesed (Mercy), the sword represents Geburah (the full penalty of the Law), and the Scales equate with the equilibrium of Tiphereth (Harmony).

The number eight on the Divine Plane signifies justice in its divine sense correlating with the principle of Balance. The number eight on the Occult Plane represents dualism, positive and negative, and the actions of unseen forces on matter. On the Material Plane the number eight stands for the mother instinct throughout Nature.

CHAPTER X

ARCANUM IX:
THE HERMIT

Arcanum IX—"The Hermit", "L' Hermite", of the Marseille Tarot, illustrates an adult bearded man in monastic garb, proceeding it would seem with caution to some known destination. In his right hand he carries a lantern lit by a small flame, and in his left hand a pilgrim's staff. The Hermit is not a strict anchorite for quite obviously he has no plans to sit in meditation in a cave, but is bent on exploring the outer world with which he is as yet unfamiliar. He therefore commences his journey with prudence and cautiously, knowing full well that he will have to overcome unaccustomed obstacles which he will meet. He is Hermes or the Magus now in the role of a hermit, the androgynous young man of Arcanum VI — "The Lovers", who has grown to maturity both physi-

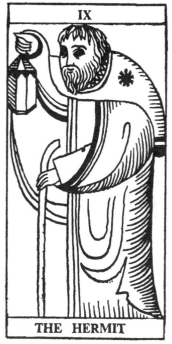

cally, spiritually, and experience-wise. Arcanum IX links with Arcanum XVI—"The Lightning-struck Tower", in terms of obstacles encountered; and with Arcanum XI—"The Enchantress" or "Strength", in terms of his resolution when he successfully overcomes life's hazards. He ultimately reaches the peak of his

37

attainment at the time of the subsequent maturation of his initiatory experiences through sacrifice, as pictorially represented in
Arcanum XII—"The Hanged Man", when the futility of search-
ing for Wisdom with artificial aids becomes very obvious. The
light carried by the Hermit is the Light of Hermes Trismegistus,
the Lantern of Intellect, the Spark Divine. The Mage Eliphas
Levi from the storehouse of his Arcane knowledge states that the
Hermit's mantle is that of Apollonius of Tyana. The Hermit's
staff is doubtlessly the Staff of Righteousness on which he leans
for support. (c.f. King Arthur's Excalibur on a more militant
plane.)

The Hermit then is Man in search of himself, pursuing the
lonely Path of the awakened soul in its search for Truth, guided
by his lantern and guarded by his staff. In essence, Arcanum IX
represents Self-initiatory experience which is threefold in as much
as the Hermit fortified by the Wisdom obtained from "Isis"—
Arcanum II, is enabled to enter the "Silence" where he experiences the Astral Light (a State of Consciousness), and by so
doing discovers the true relationship between himself and the
rest of humanity, and is in rapport with the Lords of Light
and the Shining Ones, by reason of his Spiritual Awareness.
Nine is the number of Initiation, which commences in Yesod the
Ninth Sephira of the Kabala, which is the world of forms built
up out of the substance of the Astral Ether, that living primordial
substance, a condition of the Astral Light, the substance which
constitutes the basis of all form life. The downpouring of the
great creative forces of the Universe via the Astral Light, mater-
ialises on the plane of dense physical matter. From the higher
levels of the Astral Light proceed those great spiritual upsurges
which regenerate mankind; whilst perverted life-force of a malig-
nant nature stems from the semi-intelligent forces of the lower
astral, seeking union and materialisation with the evil image
building minds of unworthy men, and with the astral simulacra
of evils past, which exist in the Akasha, the Great spatial Astral
Void, the notebook containing the Akashic Records.

The number nine on the Divine Plane stands for Wisdom
and "The Silence". Nine on the Occult Plane represents the Astral
Light, the matrix of all form life. On the material Plane nine is
indicative of protection in human affairs, and can also signify
either of the opposing emotions of human love or hate.

"Who never wins can rarely lose,
 Who never climbs as rarely falls."

(Whittier)

CHAPTER XI

ARCANUM X:
THE WHEEL OF FORTUNE

Arcanum X — "The Wheel of Fortune", or "La roue de Fortune" of the Marseille Tarot, illustrates a large wheel at the top of which apparently seated in a pose of equilibrium is the Egyptian god Osiris, crowned and sworded. Facing the card, on the right side of the wheel, is Hermanubis the jackal-headed god attempting to ascend to the top of the wheel, and on the left side of the wheel is Typhon or Set, the evil genius of Egyptian mythology, in the process of being thrown off from the wheel's rim with his head pointing downwards. The Egyptians represented Typhon as a wolf, but in the card he looks more like a monkey or a caricature of a man's face: in any event the Egyptians held him responsible for all of the world's evils.

WHEEL OF LIFE

In various Tarot packs the three figures on the wheel differ. Sometimes the Sphinx is shown at the top of the wheel symbolising the eternal riddle of Creation. In the great Italian Tarot we have a male and female figure seated at the top of the wheel apparently in a state of contentment; a nude blindfolded female figure rotates the wheel, whilst a man is seen being cast off from the right side of the wheel (facing one), over the edge of a precipice. The esoteric meaning of the Italian Tarot Trump No. X is no different, though the symbology is more imaginative but less esoterically correct. The Wheel of Fortune has been correlated with the Zodiacal circle which forms the background of the motions of the Sun, Moon and other planets, and accordingly with Man's Samsaric earthly existence, his evolutionary cycle from birth to death, till finally liberation (Paramamukti) is attained, when his Karma is paid in full.

Arcanum X stresses the active participation of Man the Microcosm in as much as he must focus his inward eye on himself the closed system, and use his psychic powers to control his life, rather than be controlled by it (c.f. the quest for the Holy Grail in the Arthurian legends). The androgynous young man of Arcanum VI—"The Lovers", dismounting as a King from his chariot (Arcanum VII—The Chariot) now enjoys a spiritual triumph, having realised that the vicissitudes of fate are not as fickle as they seem, further, that the Wheel of Fate (Fortune) is not destiny itself, but one of its many instruments, for all influences and their processes are reciprocal. This reciprocality is the basis of the Kabalistic Tree of Life as applied to the human pentagram.

The Hermeticism of the Kabala premises to seek the true essence of Being in everything with which we come into contact, and to elucidate the transition from the infinite to the finite. The Kabalistic Tree of Life posits that there are ten numbered manifestations of everything called the Ten Sephiroth (Singular—Sephira), or "Spheres" or Emanations, namely, ten aspects on the Tree of Life. The Archetype for the ten Sephiroth is "Ain Soph —The Absolute, the Inaccessible, the Unknowable. Evolutionary escalation from Sephira to Sephira can only be through the paths of Astral power. The Ten Sephiroth are as follows—

I Kether (The Crown). The idea of knowledge. The supreme emanation.

II Chocmah (Wisdom). Desire of cognition (theoretical).

III Binah (Mind). The Knower or Understanding (practical).

IV Chesed (Will). Grace, Charity, Love.

V Geburah. Intelligence.

VI Tiphereth. Beauty or Harmony.

VII Netzah. Justice or Victory.

VIII Hod. Glory or Peace.

IX Yesod (Form). Forms in general. Foundation. Base.

X Malkuth (World). Kingship, Kingdom. The germ of the material world of concrete form in which we live.

The diagram of the Kabalistic Tree of Life reproduced below, strictly speaking belongs to the theoretical Kabala.

THE ABSOLUTE AIN SOPH

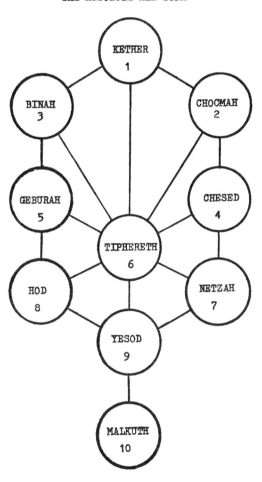

The Ten Sephiroth when correlated with the human body, represent the Archetypal or Perfect Man, each Sephira indicating that part of the body which is subject to its influence.

The Ten Sephiroth link with the Ten Names of God, the Ten classes of Angels, and the Ten members of the human body, as tabulated below:—

The Ten Sephiroth	The Ten Names of God	The Ten Classes of Angels	The Ten Members of the Human Body
1 Kether	Ehyeh (Exod. iii. 14)	Hayyôth	Head
2 Chocmah	Yâh (Isa. xxvi 4)	Ophannîm	Brain
3 Binah	Yhwh (Isa. xxvi 4)	Arêlîm (Isa. xxxiii. 7)	Heart
4 Chesed	El, the Mighty One	Hashmâlîm (Ezek. i. 4)	Right Arm
5 Geburah	Eloah	Serâphîm (Isa. vi. 6)	Left Arm
6 Tiphereth	Elohîm	Shinanîm	Chest
7 Netzah	Jehovah Sabâôth	Tarshîshîm Dan. x. 6)	Right Leg
8 Hod	Elohîm Sabâôth	Sons of God (Gen. vi. 4)	Left Leg
9 Yesod	El Hayy, the Mighty Living One	Ishîm (Ps. civ. 4)	Genital Organs
10 Malkuth	Adônâi, the Lord	Cherûbîm	Union of the Whole Body

The greatest of the names of God was YHWH, the so-called Tetragammaton, which was never pronounced and only written.

In the Kabala, the Gnosis, or secret traditional knowledge there are three divisions of the ten Sephiroth, each division representing a different aspect of the same divinity, or put in another way a triune division representing the Intellectual World, the world of Perception, and the Material or Physical world. The three divisions grouped together represent an indivisible Trinity. The first three Sephira indicate the first Manifestation of God, are metaphysically intellectual in content, expressing the absolute identity of existence, thought, and form. The second grouped division of three Sephira identify God as an aspect of supreme goodness and wisdom, and as the origin of beauty in all her manifestations in creation. In the last three Sephira, God is identified as the primal cause and generative principle underlying the world of nature, to wit, the symbol of concretion in the natural world. At the top of the Tree of Life is Ain-Soph, the No-Thing, the Great Unknown, the "Ancient of Days", who presides over the triune aspects of Divinity, to be correlated with the mystical triad "AUM" of the Vedas. It should be observed that the Kabalistic triad becomes less metaphysical as it descends in order to conform and gain acceptance by human intelligence at lower levels. In its final analysis the triple triad in the Tree of Life is such that the three male Sephira are on the right, the three female on the left, and the four principles of Unity in the centre. In every triad there is a male, female and an androgyne.

The Kabala therefore is a metaphysical system to enable the elect to know God and the Universe, by a comprehension of the divine through speculation, pre-supposing that in this way we can grasp the fundamental ideas in respect of the plan of the world architecture. The ten Sephiroth are contained in Adam Kadmon the Primordial Man. Perhaps this was in effect Paul's reference in Corinthians which reads—"God created a heavenly Adam in the spiritual world and an earthly Adam of clay for the material world." This in an overall sense lines up with the tenets of Plato and Zoroaster, both of whom held that things and beings exist as ideas before they are materially created, bringing the practical Kabala into the field of Magic whereby through the ritual of spoken words marvellous results are manifested in the world of matter. "Words do not fall into the void." (Sefer Zohar—The Book of Splendour).

In Arcane terminology "The Wheel of Fortune" is sometimes

referred to as "The Wheel of Ezekiel"—(c.f. Ezekiel Chapter 1). Tarot-wise, I am unable in my present state of ignorance to reconcile this description of Arcanum X with a fiery sphere as described by Ezekiel which appeared out of a whirlwind from the North, other than as an U.F.O. Briefly: in 593 B.C. an U.F.O. (very accurately described by the prophet in the non-technical language of his day) landed close to the Chebar River in Chaldea (Iraq). The prophet also saw the figure of a man surrounded with a blinding light. Ezekiel was taken on board the craft and transported to the Tel Abib mountains where he was left: he remained "speechless" for seven days. The preciseness of the prophet's description of the U.F.O. belies any chicanery on his part savouring of imaginative saucery.

The number ten on the Divine Plane stands for Potential force; on the Occult Plane for magic power, predestination, and Karma, for actions which are inevitable, and stands impartially for either good or evil and is always arbitrary; on the Material Plane ten represents luck, chance, and Karma.

"The Wheel of Fortune turns incessantly round, and who can say within himself, I shall today be uppermost!"

(Confucius)

CHAPTER XII

ARCANUM XI:
THE ENCHANTRESS

Arcanum XI, "The Enchantress', "La Force" of the Marseille Tarot, depicts a young woman either opening or closing the jaws of a lion, apparently without fear or effort. Arcanum XI links with Arcanum I—"The Magus", for the first enlightenment of the Magus is manifest in Arcanum XI as the Divine Will in operation, namely, the ascendancy of spiritual over physical power, whereby the Enchantress* conquers the Gnostic Lion-Serpent, Nahash the Guardian of the Threshold, a strictly Aquarian principle, for eleven is the number of the Aquarian Age. The Solar activity of Leo, namely, the operative will power of the querent is now under control by his spiritual intelligence. Arcanum XI also links with Arcanum XIII—"The Reaper", in as much as the transmutation of vital force to spiritual courage is implied by inference. The Conquered-Lion symbology, Solar in essence, together with

XI

THE ENCHANTRESS

---

* c.f. Spencer's symbology of Una and the Lion.

the shape of the hat brim which resembles a figure eight lying on its side (c.f. Arcanum I—"The Magus", for a hat of similar shape and design), indicates that the woman (feminine and Lunar in aspect) is applying spiritual rather than physical force in subjugating her lion, lion-serpent, or dragon, namely, the Sun as Logos, or in its Zodiacal place as Leo. To express the same idea in a more empirical way, the immanent and transcendent Divine Will must be in control everywhere.

The Enchantress, an androgynous Hermetic Aquarian symbol of Virgo the mother, the Eternal She, is now in control of the vital force Prana by conquering the Gnostic lion-serpent, and thereby strengthens and consolidates her position. The original Seeker who started out as the Magus in Arcanum I, became the androgynous young Man or Arcanum VI—"The Lovers", and the kingly charioteer of Arcanum VII, now receives the full benefit of Prana the vital force at a lower vibration level, so that it can be accepted and distributed if needs be on the third-dimensional earth-plane, as an aid to the working of Samsara, the evolutionary cycle from birth to death.

The Enchantress has often been likened to the female equivalent of St. George and the Dragon. In the calendar of Saints there have been several other dragon-slayers. This dragon symbolism has been preserved in the folklore of many nations with an esoteric meaning that remains fundamentally the same. Yet another aspect of the symbology would be the conquest of the carnal urges, the fiery passions of Leo, resulting in balance and harmony (Arcanum VIII) of the two opposing natures of man, assisted by the Divine Wisdom of Isis—Arcanum II.

The number eleven on the Divine Plane signifies Universal energy—Prana; on the Occult Plane spiritual will power in the astral; and on the Material Plane, vitality or intense strength.

"He holds no parley with unmanly fears;
  Where duty bids, he confidently steers,
  Faces a thousand dangers at her call,
  And, trusting in his God, surmounts them all."

(Cowper)

CHAPTER XIII

ARCANUM XII:
THE HANGED MAN

Arcanum XII — "The Hanged Man", "Le Pendu" of the Marseille Tarot, is the most spiritual of the whole Tarot. Illustrated is a man hanging upside-down by his left foot with his right leg crossed behind the left, from a species of gibbet. Each of the side posts of the gibbet has six lopped branches along its length. The man's arms are held akimbo behind his back forming an inverted triangle, the total aspect being that of an inverted triangle surmounted by a cross, thus $\begin{smallmatrix}+\\\nabla\end{smallmatrix}$
The inverted triangle is the alchemical sigil for water and the cross the end product or consummation of the Great Work of the Adept. However, the man, the same figure as in Arcanum I and Arcanum VI, is not being hanged in the literal context of "hanging" as a punishment for a capi-

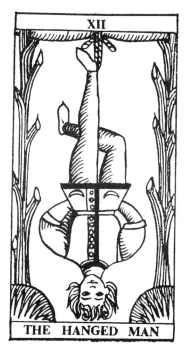

THE HANGED MAN

tal offence, but would appear to be rather an entranced Adept suspended as it were, in transition between lives, "the dark night of the soul", when TRUTH stands verily naked before the as yet spiritually unprepared and immature mind of the querent. The man's eyes are opened and are gazing skywards for the vision of things celestial, and if he has not yet completed his Samsaric

49

D

journey he is almost at his goal of liberation, Paramamukti. A Jivanmukti he already is, namely, a potential Adept as yet earth-bound. All that is now required is the maturation of his initiatory experiences during his Samsaric suspension or transition between lives, or alternatively, he has no further need to qualify through fresh incarnations through any of the twelve signs of the Zodiac represented by the six lopped branches on each of the side-supports of the gibbet.

This indeed is the Rose and the Cross, the 18th Hermetic degree of the Rosy-Cross conferred in Freemasonry in so far as the esoteric aspect is high-lighted. The Cross represents both Generation and Regeneration, being at once the beginning and end, for—"In Cruce salus". The two-fold aspect of the cross is one in essence, namely, Wisdom and Love. The two transverse beams of the cross symbolise the character of perfection, the at-one-ment between the Divine and human wills. The Crux Ansata or handle cross, the cross of Osiris was the most sacred symbol of Egyptian antiquity, indicating the path to eternal life. Says A. E. Waite: "The Cross is a hierogram of, if possible still higher antiquity than the floral emblem", the Rose, and is in any event more universal. The Rose the symbol of beauty and life, in the words of Eliphas Levi, "expressed in a mystical manner all the protestations of the Renaissance. It was the flesh revolting against the oppression of the spirit, it was Nature declaring herself to be, like grace, the daughter of God; it was love refusing to be stifled by the celibate, it was life desiring to be no longer barren, it was humanity aspiring to a natural religion, full of love and reason, founded on the revelation of the harmonies of existence of which the Rose was for Initiates the living and blooming symbol . . . The conquest of the Rose was the problem offered by Initiation and science, while religion toiled to prepare and establish the universal, exclusive, and definitive triumph of the Cross." Supreme Initiation implies the union of the Rose and the Cross, which the Neophyte-like "Le Pendu" must work out for himself, including the Mystery of the Rose which will never be known to anyone except the Adept and cannot be therefore described.

The potential, prudent Adept of Arcanum IX—"The Hermit", has freed himself from the Wheel of Rebirth—Arcanum X, and has now been raised to glory through the equation and harmony between his higher and lower self. Bhagawan, the concept of a personal God, is in essence no different to the realisation of Atman the Self of self, the Spark Divine deep in the heart chakra of man. "Le Pendu", "The Hanged Man"—Arcanum XII represents the elevated potential Adept of Arcanum IX—the Hermit, who now has nine more paths of progression before the Great Transmutation of Arcanum XXI is accomplished.

The number twelve* on the Divine Plane signifies Sacrifice; on the Occult Plane signifies Immortality and the Elixir of Life; and on the Material Plane represents Bondage.

"Heaven's harmony is universal love."

(Cowper)

* THE NUMBER TWELVE AND THE ZODIAC

The Zodiac is the symbolic allegory of the Cycle of the Sun, both physically and spiritually. The Sun "the Jewel in the Lotus" of the Zodiac, radiates its white light to each sign of the zodiac, portraying twelve aspects of the Spiritual Sun, and makes the zodiac the great Circle of Manifestation within which the created universe appears. The physical Sun lights, warms the heart, and imparts the Spark Divine in man.

The Karmic implications of the number twelve are aboundantly clear, for the Soul must incarnate at different times under each of the twelve signs, not infrequently many times under a particular sign to suit the specific and varying needs of the incarnating Soul. There is no set incarnating order, say from Aries to Pisces on the road to Cosmic Consciousness.

In terms of Spiritual Alchemy, Eliphas Levi wrote—"The great work is, before all things, the creation of man by himself, that is to say, the full and entire conquest of his faculties and his future." And the final words from Madame Blavatsky—"Humanity and the stars are bound together indissolubly, because of the Intelligences that rule the latter."

CHAPTER XIV

ARCANUM XIII:
THE REAPER

Arcanum XIII of the Marseille Tarot is un-named on the card, but is commonly referred to as "The Reaper" or as "Death". From the aspect of anatomy, a badly drawn and rather off-putting human skeleton is shown in the act of cutting with a scythe. At the skeleton's feet lie a scattering of human heads, feet and in particular one upraised dismembered hand. Arcanum XIII is the most practical and useful for everyone, and is in fact the very natural and logical sequel to Arcanum XII—"Le Pendu". Now the entranced upside-down Hanged Man is subjected to the further processes of Generation and Regeneration, pointing as before to the Samsaric Death-birth cycle which ceases only when full liberation has been attained. The more naive esoteric interpretation comes readily to mind without much mental effort, namely, that physical death is no respector of persons, of wealth, or of age. However, it is only in this esoteric frame of reference that this interpretation rings true. In the miscellany of human heads, feet, and hands, on which the Reaper is about to use his scythe, the eyes of the two human heads are open, and seem to

be intensely alive. The other dismembered human extremities also seem to be animated rather than lifeless, and are reaching upwards towards the light. It should be observed in passing, that the sickle or curved blade was a very ancient phallic symbol.

Esoterically symbolised we have the duality of Creator and Destroyer (c.f. Brahma the Creator and Siva the Destroyer in the same context), with Regeneration as the prime end-product. Phoenix-wise we are born in spirit again after the soul has been shut off for a time from the Divine Light, namely, the "Dark Night of the Soul", the period of darkness (the Moon) and despair when in between incarnations the Soul as yet spiritually unprepared, experiences the anguish of having to view TRUTH unveiled. However, this would only constitute negative Samsaric experience of a relatively temporary nature. More Arcanely, the man is sloughing off all the carnal urges of his old self. The involuntionary road to perfection sought by "Le Pendu", is now subjected to evolutionary processes which will be equilibrated and harmonised by the catalyst Maya, for at this level of spiritual progression and consciousness, Maya will indeed be seen to be Illusion. Mouni Sadhu has very aptly said—"The best preparation for death is a WELL-SPENT LIFE."

Arcanum XIII is sometimes referred to as the "Lord of the Gates", correlated also to the number thirteen, where the Gates represent Light and Darkness, Day and Night, and Life and Death. The "Years of the Gates" are those years when the number thirteen crops up in human affairs, and especially when the sum total of year and age adds up to thirteen. At this stage then, the "boundary" point or "Year of the Gate" is reached and personal affairs are terminated. The number thirteen is neither lucky nor unlucky when considered by itself.

The number thirteen* on the Divine Plane signifies the Divine,

---

* THE NUMBER THIRTEEN AND THE ZODIAC

The number thirteen symbolises the Sun in the centre of the twelve signs of the zodiac as the Manifestation of the physical Universe in as much as the true Adept has to pass through the twelve trials of Initiation which correspond to the twelve zodiacal signs. Herein lies the key to the multiple legends of Saviour Gods, exemplifying the Law of Cyclic

the Creator; on the Occult Plane it signifies transformations in
the vegetable, mineral, human, and astral worlds; and on the
Material Plane, thirteen generally represents a change for the
better or in any event for new birth: it also stands for the Earth
function of woman.

> "Gather the rosebuds while ye may,
> Old Time is still a-flying;
> And the same flower that blooms today,
> Tomorrow shall be dying."
>
> (Herrick)

Manifestation, namely the dual aspects of both the physical and Spiritual
Sun, the former in its annual journey vivifying the physical Universe, and
the latter glorifying that spiritual part of man which is indestructible. Of
such stuff are the Sun Initiates mentioned in the folk lore and legends
which survive all over the world and have manifested in every Manvantara
(cycle of expression). The descriptions of the Sun Initiates vary in metaphor
and language, but the matrix of TRUTH is the same.

As in all aspects of the Tarot, the principle of duality exists in respect
of the number thirteen. Whilst it is evocative of good, it is also negatively
evocative of evil, drawing to it all the noxious simulacra and evil astral
debris that temporarily exists in the Akashic Records or Astral Light,
referred to as the "Scarlet Woman" in Revelations XVII, 1 - 2 as follows—
"Come hither; I will shew unto thee the judgement of the great whore
that sitteth on many waters: with whom the kings of the earth have
committed fornication, and the inhabitants of the earth have been made
drunk with the wine of her fornication."

CHAPTER XV

Arcanum XIV — "Temperance" of the Marseille Tarot, often referred to as "The Angel of Time", illustrates a winged female figure pouring a liquid in a continuous stream from one vase to another, which represents the time continuum, the concept of past, present and future as aspects of the eternal present. The dual symbolism of the vases points to the Solar Angelic effect of the spiritualisation of the astral self, or in another sense the descent of Spirit into Matter in order that the progressing Adept might be inspired to think and act in terms of the Divinity of which he is a part. The wings of the angel lend force to the fact that spiritual assistance in terms of enlightenment, or spiritual fire, comes from the Solar Logos and is certainly not from this earth,

and is a manifestation of the relationship between the Above and the Below (c.f. Arcanum III—"L'Imperatrice", the female aspect of the Planetary Being, "The Empress of Nature", whose throne has a back rest of imperfectly drawn wings). The interpretation of the wings in Arcanum XV—"Le Diable", "The Black Magician", would in consequence be the antithesis of the wings of the Angel of Time.

The head ornament of the Angel consists of a central circle with five similar ones round it. If we view this as two concentric circles, we have $1+5=6$, which is the number of Venus linking Initiation with Beauty. Alternatively, the number of the card, namely, XIV, numerologically is $10+4$, which is equal to 5, the number of the divine hermaphrodite Hermes. "Temperance", or the Angel of Time therefore symbolises Hermetic harmony and equilibrium, Solar synthesis, the balancing of the forces in the manifested universe, when by unselfishly helping our fellow men, we are raised temporarily at least to the angelic level and thereby help to obliterate as much of our Karma as the sincerity of our actions warrant: yet another step on the path to final liberation, Paramamukti.

Arcanum XIV has also been referred to as the "Daughter of Reconcilers", namely, as one of those "mighty ones", an Angel of Justice who mediates between earth and the higher planes. The idea is not as far fetched as one might at first think, for up to the 6th Century A.D. the Church Fathers considered angels as physical beings. The recantation came subsequently to tie up with their hotchpotch of copious borrowings from various pseudo Pagan sources to shape their pseudo Christian religion in an initial and continuing attempt to take over the minds of men. The Old Testament has abundant references in Genesis, Isaiah, Job, and the Psalms, to visitants, namely, "messengers", "giants", "sanctified ones", "mighty ones", and "emissaries of the Lord" (God), who associated with, and even mated with "the daughters of men". Variations of this leitmotif of extra-terrestial visitors is to be found in race-memory and folklore all over the world, distorted withal by the imagination of primitive scribes. Herein lies the key to the Celestial Watchers, the extra-terrestial Vigilantes, wherein also lies the substratum, proof and starting point in any investigation conducted for the establishment of the reality of U.F.O's. But the shreds of truth and evidence extant, and in the possession of the hierarchy of various world governments cannot be made public, for man-the-irrational would panic in a measure that would confound mankind. Man in his conceit is content to complacently amble along, priding himself on the shallowness of his technological knowledge, and mentally rejects the idea that there might well be more intelligent beings than himself on planets even outside the Solar system, who belong to some other star system and have an intellectual development-rate and technological knowledge far in excess of Earthmen.

The number fourteen* on the Divine Plane signifies Involution, the descent of Spirit into Matter. On the Occult Plane fourteen represents Transmutation; and on the Material Plane fourteen stands for the activity of man in the seasons' round.

"Temperance is a bridle of gold; he who uses it rightly is more like a god than a man."

(R. Burton)

---

* Fourteen is the number of Delusions, the end of the second Septenary of the Tarot path, called in the Sepher Yetzirah the Path of Illuminating Intelligence, when the Adept must ensure that his thought forces are constructively creative in obedience to his will.

CHAPTER XVI

ARCANUM XV:
THE DEVIL

Arcanum XV of the Marseille Tarot is "Le Diable", commonly referred to as "The Devil", or the "Black Magician". Le Diable is the spurious Magus, the antithesis of Arcanum I. The Black Magician is the Seeker raised to Angelic heights in Arcanum XIV—"Temperance", who has through pride, conceit and a lust for domination, abused his newly acquired control over the Astral Light (of which more anon), and has put his magical powers to evil use, consorting with the Powers of Darkness for his own vain aggrandisement.

THE BLACK MAGICIAN

Arcanum XV illustrates an androgynous devilish figure standing on a plinth which may well be a mock throne. The figure has clawed feet and hands, a pair of stag-like horns, and wings resembling those of a bat. As opposed to the Magus of Arcanum I, the right clawed hand is raised in fiendish benediction, whilst the lowered left hand holds a flaming torch signifying his burning desire to unleash the powers of evil. Roped to the pedestal are two little horned male and female creatures, imps, who complement his own unsavoury bearing, and express the carnal urges of both sexes of mankind.

Le Diable should not be rigidly equated with the Christian Devil* or we will fail to appreciate the esoteric import of this controversial card. In some Tarot packs the Devil is represented by a figure resembling Pan the God of Nature, with the extremities of a goat, a spreader of Pan-ic, the medieval antithesis of Divinity and synonymous with the powers of Satan. And so to the break up of the Order of Knights Templar whom it is alleged paid obeisance to the goat-like god Pan representing the Powers of Darkness under the name of Baphomet if the findings and castigations of Holy Church are to be believed. Whatever may have been the inner reasons for the dissolution of the Order, it is abundantly clear that the Templars were capable of physically producing astral creations from the Astral Light, which were veiled in the word "TEMOHPAB" which is Baphomet reversed— "Templi Omnium Hominum Pacis Abbas" (The Priest of the Temple of Peace for all Men.)

Metaphysically the Astral Light is the manifestation of form acted upon by force, namely, by the creative thoughts of man. The astral substance as such is a fluidic interpenetrating "energy-substance", the vivifying force Azoth which must be harnessed; real in its own reality as a state of consciousness, and subject to dualism when manifested as the Higher Astral and the Lower Astral. The Upper Astral represents and reflects the mental and spiritual realms where dwell the Shining Ones, the Celestial Watchers. The Lower Astral is the materialisation of the Astral Light in dense physical matter, providing the basic elemental force which can either be directed and guided or mis-directed and abused in terms of idea-force, and also acts as channels of influence for the Lords of Terror who are the astral simulacra-ideas of all' the collective evils set in motion by Man from the beginning of Time. Fortunately, forms in the Astral are not per se the Astral Light but are rather the results of the image-building powers of the human mind which tend to give such forms reality when manifested in the physical world. It lies within the power of man

---

* "There is no Devil, no Evil outside mankind to produce a Devil. Satan represents metaphysically simply the reverse or the polar opposite of everything in Nature." (Blavatsky—The Secret Doctrine). He expresses the principel of duality in the Universe.

to harness this force in order either to let the terrestial dragon brutalise mankind, or court the Celestial Dragon and usher in the Parliament of Man, and Peace on Earth to men of Goodwill.

The number fifteen* on the Divine Plane signifies Destiny; on the Occult Plane, Fear! Nahash—the dragon of the threshold. On the Material Plane fifteen represents the immense force or power in the mind of man in terms of "idea-force", which ultimately affects not only the fate of the progressing Seeker, but also the fate of all mankind.

"This is the curse of every evil deed,
That, propagating still, it brings forth evil."
(Coleridge)

* The number fifteen, combining as it does the 10 of Perfection and the 5 of Humanity, finally becomes the 6 of the Christos, the life-force (1+5=6), clearly indicative that fifteen represents NOT individual man, but indeed humanity, expressing thereby the Karmic pattern of the lives of all men. No man is an island, for perfection can only be obtained by and through the Brotherhood of Man. To associate the number fifteen with the Devil is poppycock, for apart from the beliefs of organised Christianity of any complexion, there is no devil outside of man's perverted creations. Says Eliphas Levi—"In a word the devil is for us, even as mortal sin is, to our thinking, the persistence of the will in what is absurd . . . He who affirms the devil, creates or makes the devil."

CHAPTER XVII

ARCANUM XVI:
THE LIGHTNING-STRUCK
TOWER

Arcanum XVI — "La Maison Dieu" of the Marseille Tarot, "The House of God", also referred to as "The Lightning-Struck Tower", illustrates a three-windowed tower which has apparently been struck by lightning on a clear day. Two men are shown being hurled to the ground from the wrecked summit of the tower. Thirty-seven tiny circles are also shown debris-wise scattered on either side of the tower, descending earthwards. The number thirty-seven reduces numerologically to one ($37=3+7=10=1$), which is the number which represents the first principle, the Creator, the divine sign of universal life. These circles could represent the descent of the Solar Spirit into Matter. Though the circles appear to be descending they are

XVI

THE TOWER

actually relative to their placements, and represent that age-old Hermetic maxim—"As Above so Below".

The lesser interpretation of Arcanum XVI would be the fall from high estate of the spurious Mage of Arcanum XV, whom Nemesis has overtaken. This may well be so, but might not the Tower be a symbolic representation of the Seeker, of the Tower

(Temple) not made with hands, cloistered in darkness from the Heaven that lies all around us, dimly illuminated by the three tiny windows, now suddenly struck by the effulgent light that marks the onset of the illumination of the Initiate. This surely is the state of Jivanmukti* when the Adept's living body now becomes the House of God. The beatifical illumination is always that sudden flash of Eternal Sunlight on the target area of the heart. In the same sense, the struck Tower could also represent an advanced Adept who having attained Jivanmukti, now awaits complete liberation, Paramamukti, from the bondage of the flesh and the Samsaric round.

In the negative aspect the struck Tower represents "the dark night of the soul", when the spiritually unprepared and immature querent is confronted to his utter confusion by TRUTH stripped of all her vestments. In this negative aspect, Le Maison Dieu has also been referred to as the "Fall of the Angels", the fall or descent being in terms of the Seeker's "fall from grace" in Arcanum XV, because of his own errors and consequent Karmic repercussions, or by the misuse of his free will. Self deceived, he will not admit that his knowledge is limited and fails to realise that he cannot deceive the Immanent and Transcendent God. The spurious Mage in his attempts to control the astral for selfish or unworthy ends, generates a Nahash type of astral current triggering FATE, and whilst he preserves some astral forms, he destroys others at the same time.

The number sixteen on the Divine Plane signifies Divine destruction; on the Occult Plane sixteen signifies the fall of man, and alchemically stands for calcination. On the Material Plane sixteen is never a good number, and represents alterations, changes and disappointments. When linked with the number eighteen, "sixteen" represents financial losses or a loss in prestige and power.

> "When God shuts the door,
> He opens a window."
>
> (Anon.)

---

* In the number 16, the 10 of perfection plus the 6 of the Christ-force, finds its ultimate in 7 ($16 = 1 + 6 = 7$), the victory and manifestation of Perfection on earth, namely, Jivanmukti.

CHAPTER XVIII

Arcanum XVII of the Marseille Tarot, "L'Etoile", The Star, depicts a nude young woman in what appears to be a state of meditation, kneeling on one knee by a stream, where she is emptying the contents of two vases (one held in each hand), to wit, the Elixir of Life, into the running water. The Elixir of Life flowing from the two vases is the dual Pranic stream of Ida (the feminine aspect), and Pingala (the male aspect), which unite under the right conditions in the region of the spinal column in terms of Kundalini or Serpent-fire. Near the woman a butterfly is sometimes illustrated, resting upon a flower, representing the soul upon the Kabalistic Tree of Life. A scarlet Ibis, the Egyptian bird sacred to the Great Hermes is in some Tarot packs shown seated

on a bush, representing the Wisdom of the Silence as an aid to meditation for a glimpse of the Truth that lies beyond. In other words, the young woman by meditation is bringing into practice the Rosicrucian injunction of "TRY" against the backdrop of her subconscious (the stream whose flow she is augmenting), which in point of fact represents in a collective sense the stream of universal consciousness, agitated into activity by the meditations of the sincere Seekers of Truth.

It is not surprising therefore, that Trump XVII has also been referred to as "The Dweller between the Waters", linking with Arcanum I—The Magus, with the feminine affinities in Trump III —Mother Nature, with Trump II—Isis, and with Trump XI—The Enchantress or "La Force" who overcomes the Lion-Serpent or Nahash.

Above the kneeling woman's head are seven eight-pointed stars, symbols of Solar energy impinging beneficent rays on the enlightened Adept. The artist of "L'Etoile" would appear to have sacrificed exactness of representation in respect of the seven stars on the altar of Art, for the stars in question relate directly to Man the Seeker, and should therefore be upright pentagrams indicative of Man's septenary nature, namely, Rupa the physical body; Prana, Cosmic energy or force; Linga Sharira, the astral double or the Mage's Magnum Opus; MANAS, the dual principle of Mind, i.e. the higher and lower intelligence; and Atman the Godhead in man attained in the state of Samadhi. An eighth larger star is immediately above the woman's head, the Star of the Magi which also ought to be an upright pentagram, which indicates the challenge presented by Aquarian youth in an attempt to revitalise the earth. Two other aspects of star symbology can also be read into the placement of the eight stars above the head of the kneeling Aquarian woman. Firstly, on the healing plane the large star stands for the transference of the Life Force in terms of the born and destined healer. The seven lesser stars represent secondary healers. Secondly, the grouped stars premise the central truth of Astrology, namely, "Astra inclinant non necessitant!"—The stars incline but do not compel.

"L'Etoile" therefore represents the Samsaric earth position of the querent, who none the less is fortified by Hope in the shape of "The Dweller between the Waters", who is a link between the "Waters Above" and the "Waters Below". The Star symbolises Cosmic forces of all kinds, of most of which we are as yet completely ignorant. These Cosmic forces have their origin in the Immanent and Transcendent, and function throughout the world. The Star partially expresses their manifestation. This particular symbology is carried further and brought to fruition in the Unnumbered card, when Cosmic Consciousness is manifested in the

Magus of Arcanum I, completing the transition and transmutation between Human and Divine, as the Hope of the Aquarian Age. The essence and spirit of Arcanum XVII is hidden in that childhood jingle which begins—"Twinkle, twinkle little star . . ." etc., where if for "star" we substitute "wisdom", the message becomes clearer: it is the message of Hope fired by our conscience and powered by our intuition, in which Aquarian youth will be the pioneers and the torch-bearers.

On the Divine Plane the number seventeen signifies Wisdom and Immortality; on the Occult Plane it represents spiritual intelligence; and on the Material Plane it stands for Intellect, hope and happiness, and is the symbol of speech.

> "The stars are mansions built by Nature's hand,
> And, haply, there the spirits of the blest
> Dwell, clothed in radiance, their immortal rest."
>   (Wordsworth)

CHAPTER XIX

ARCANUM XVIII:
THE MOON

Late Autumnal shadows
And the cry of 'Horse and
    Hattock!'
Herne* the Hunter passeth by.
Stern guardian of the dark forest
When the wind is high,
Heralded by earthly dogs
Baying to a leaden sky.
Samiatz† raised to pristine state
A just and vengeful shadow did
    create.
Pursue on till time eternal
Till thy work is done,
All those who would despoil
The Brotherhood of Man.

          ("Herne the Hunter"
          by C. A. PUSHONG, 1961)

THE MOON

    Trump XVIII of the Marseille Tarot—"La Lune" or "The Moon", presents something of an enigma, for it has been sagely and strangely interpreted by various cartomancers. The overall depressing suggestiveness of the

---

* Traditionally, Herne was a Forest Warden at Windsor in the reign of Henry VIII. He was also a poacher. To avoid disgrace he hanged himself from an oak tree which his ghost is said to haunt in the form of a great stag, whenever disaster faces the nation or the royal family.

symbology does little at first glance to enlighten the querent. In the lower part of the illustration we see a Crayfish, a Piscean sigil, endeavouring to rise from the darkness of the primeval slime to the dry land where there is light. The analogy to the querent's ascent to yet another level in his spiritual progression is quite apparent. The remainder of the card shows two dogs (and not a dog and a wolf as indicated in some Tarot packs) similar in appearance, howling at the Moon, or rather at the old Moon embraced by the new moon. The Moon's magnetism preserves and generates life, and the dogs here are undoubtedly Hecate's, the goddess of the Moon's darker aspect. However, as with all lunar goddesses who have a dual aspect, the dogs may well have Diana of the Chase as their mistress. The dogs are flanked by two towers indicative of the boundaries of the material world as against the boundless Celestial kingdom. The Moon therefore symbolises the reflected rays of the subconscious, and the eighteen flame-like tongues of light falling from the Moon represent the descent of Spirit into Matter, with the Seeker in the early stages of spiritual enlightenment represented by the ascending Crayfish.

The moral of Trump XVIII is that when the creative imagination is put into practice for useful or concrete purposes, the end product must be good. Alternatively, the querent would become enmeshed in the grip of delusory forces and would become a purveyor of poppycock, for man becouse of his stupidity and lack of inner vision comes into conflict with the occult hierarchy in as much as he contravenes the Hierarchic Law. The medieval escape from the evils of the world to "heaven" as portrayed in Arcanum XVIII is a misrepresentation which probably stems from the medieval Church. The Piscean sigil of the Crayfish clearly indicates the ascension from "the dark night of the soul" towards the Light (Astral), and rebirth. Hecate's howling dogs cease to terrify with

---

† Samiatz was originally one of the fallen angels who later recanted and was forgiven by God.

"The Fallen Angels, so called, are Humanity itself . . . The Fallen Angels, in every ancient system are made the prototypes of fallen men— allegorically, and those men themselves—esoterically." (Blavatsky)

"The Angels aspire to become Men; for the perfect Man, the Man-God is above even Angels." (Eliphas Levi)

the opening of the Neptunian Third Eye, the eye of Shiva. The darkness of Maya is now seen in terms of the Light of Reality, namely, as having positive reality to the mind in which the Third eye begins to function. Of such stuff is the First Initiation.

The number eighteen on the Divine Plane signifies Chaos, the final point of evolution; on the Occult Plane eighteen indicates spiritual hindrances and also the fall in grace of the soul; whilst on the Material Plane eighteen represents Matter, and is always a sign of trouble, anxiety, failure, hidden enemies, and hidden dangers in general.

CHAPTER XX

ARCANUM XIX:
THE SUN

The interpretation of Arcanum XIX—"Le Soleil", The Sun, offers a challenge, for little of any significant worth has been said by most occultists which would even be understandable to the average querent who hopes to get an insight into the esoteric structure of the Tarot. The symbolism depicted on the card is in a sense misleading, for we see at the top of the card a radiant Sun transmitting its rays earthwards which finally narrow to a cascade of thirteen tongues of Solar fire descending on two almost naked identical children who are standing before a brick wall. The Sun is the Solar Logos acting in concert with higher powers, who is transmitting life-giving emanations to all forms of manifest life on earth with special reference to man the immortal, in order that

THE SUN

he may regenerate or renew his consciousness, awakening his personality with a view to kindling the Spark Divine, the Atman or Self. The twins have no apparent connexion with the Zodiacal sign of Gemini, but illustrate the principle of ambivalence in the concept of duality, which is the recurrent theme in the Major Arcana of the Tarot.

The correlation here is between Trump XIX and Arcanum XI (The Enchantress—"La Force"), and with Trump I—The Magus. The querent having proceeded along the Tarot paths by Fortitude and Sacrifice, and equipped with the Solar power of the Gnostic Lion (Divine Wisdom), now nears his journey's end, having reached the fifth stage of his yet incomplete Adeptship. He is as yet naked like a little child, although he is freed from the limitations of physical mater and is a Jivanmukti waiting for final liberation—Paramamukti. The Jivanmukti has succeeded in separating the subtle from the gross with the assistance of the Astral Light—Azoth. With the opening of the Third Eye and complete identification with life here and now, the Adept is able to differentiate between the physical self and the mental individual that he is, and entertains the hope and possibility of a life or lives yet to come in a higher state of being. Both the wall and the semi-naked children further substantiate the querent's earth-bound Jivanmuktiship, for he is now blessed by the effulgent and regenerative rays of the Solar Logos, having won a complete spiritual victory over his gross physical self.

From what has already been said of Trump XIX in respect of the querent's fifth initiation on the road towards complete Adeptship, both the Divine and Occult significance of the number nineteen* tend to merge into one another in terms of the near fusion of Brahman and Atman in the person of the Jivanmukti. On the Material Plane the number nineteen heralds the commencement of any matter. However, in a Tarot spread Trump XIX read conjoined with Arcanum XVI—The Lightning-Struck Tower, foreshadows trouble through enemies; but read conjoined with Trump XI—The Enchantress, presages a well-earned term of prosperity.

"The glorious Sun
Stays in his course and plays the alchemist,
Turning with splendour of his precious eye
The meagre cloddy earth to glittering gold."
                    (Shakespeare—King John)

---

* The number nineteen (19=1+9=10=1) is the number of the Sun Initiate.

CHAPTER XXI

Trump XX "Le Judgement"—
The Last Judgement, illustrates
a Hebraic and Medieval concept
of the Last Judgement when
taken literally. Three naked figures, namely, a man and a
woman, with a child in the centre
are shown rising from a grave,
with the child's back facing the
viewer. High above the heads of
the three, an angel with a halo
looks out amidst a blaze of light
from a luminous cloud and is
blowing a trumpet. To the trumpet is attached a small flag
marked with a simple cross which
indicates the now complete correlation of the celestial with the
terrestial in the personal consciousness of the adept who has
reached his Sixth Initiation as a
prelude to complete Adeptship
which was the target at which
the Magus in Arcanum I had set

his sights. The personal consciousness of the adept is now on the
verge of communion with the universal consciousness for he has
entered the fourth dimension which frees him from the delusions
of Maya. To him Isis is now completely unveiled and he has
obtained his freedom from the Samsaric round and is ready to be
absorbed into **Brahma** from whence he came. This is confirmed by

71

the symbology of the child whose back is towards us.

The man represents self-consciousness, the woman subconsciousness; and the child, the regenerated and synthesised personality of the adept made manifest, for his personality now has no separate existence. In the esoteric sense the Last Judgement does not mean or refer to a final or universal judgement. The Earth-traveller is called to judgement many times by the inexorable workings of Karma. We come naked into the world and leave it naked, and the only yardstick by which we are judged is our code of behaviour, for we are always summoned by the Angel of Reason to arrive at a subjective judgement within its own particular frame of reference. The Hebraic Angel Gabriel trumpeting the Last Judgement is hardly likely to be accepted by anyone with uncommon commonsense, for it is a known fact that the early Christian Church fathers ruled that angels were spirit forms, only from the sixth century onwards. Prior to this it was common acceptance at all levels of intelligence, that angels were extraterrestial physical beings, visitants from beyond, the Great Ones, the Shining Ones. The sound of the angelic horn (trumpet) symbolises the call of the Archtype in us, sparking our inherent Divinity, making for astral transformation through varying forms of incarnations, till Jivanmukti is attained by victory over ourselves before the end of our incarnations.

Trump XX links conclusively with Arcanum II—The High Priestess or Isis; and with Arcanum XI—The Enchantress or "La Force". In terms of numerology, each of these three Trumps reduces to the digit two, and their triune fusion results in the now absolute identity between the soul of the earth personified by the Adept, and the soul of the universe: this indeed is Jivanmukti.

"What is justice?
To give every man his own."
(Aristotle)

CHAPTER XXII

ARCANUM XXI:
THE WORLD

"Le Monde", Arcanum XXI, known also as "The World", is the last numbered trump of the Marseille Tarot Major Arcana. This card is often called "The Universe", in terms of dual consciousness on both the terrestial and cosmic planes. Lecomte du Nouy in his inimitable way expressed much the same train of thought when he wrote—"The destiny of man is not limited to his existence on earth and he must never forget that fact." Illustrated is a nude figure patently hermaphrodite, with a floating veil falling across the lower part of the body, the visible upper body being female in form. The figure is surrounded by an elliptical laurel wreath which is quite in context, for the ellipse is a zero sign and symbolically represents superconsciousness. A short wand is held in each hand, that in the right hand standing for involution and that in the left hand for evolution. The wands also symbolise the Solar and Lunar attractions, for each man is his own Sun and his own Zodiac revolves around his personality. The Sun is the inner radiant centre, and the Moon acts as mediator between the Sun or Spirit, and the other spheres.

73

Round the laurel wreath at the clock positions of one, five, seven and eleven o' clock, are the heads of an eagle, a lion, a bull, and a man or angelic being, respectively. These symbols were plagiarised initially by the prophet Ezekiel and were four symbolic beings which in his visions supported the throne of Jehovah, and were in fact the Chaldeo-Babylonian protecting genii (Cherubim) of the idolatrous Babylonians and Assyrians. Later these four symbols were borrowed by Christianity via St. John. These four symbols have been equated with a number of manifestations which occur in groups of four. The commonest of these are:—

Symbols	Elements	Seasons	Zodiac Signs	Suits of the Minor Arcana
Eagle	Air	Autumn	Scorpio	Wands or Sceptres
Lion	Fire	Summer	Leo	Swords
Bull	Earth	Spring	Taurus	Pentacles
Man/Angel	Water	Winter	Aquarius	Cups

With special reference to the dancing androgyne it should be observed that the rhythm of the dance parallels the dance of Shiva (Saturn), and represents the upward ascent on the Aquarian Path as a prelude to the resumption of an androgynous state in the Sixth Race yet to come, similar to that which existed in the Third Race. It will further be observed from the placement of the legs of the figure, that the left leg is crossed behind the right one, quite the opposite to the representation in Trump XII—"The Hanged Man". The right foot in Trump XXI is however, firmly on the ground, indicating that the ego of the querent in Arcanum I—"The Magus", has advanced from material to mental, and from mental to spiritual conditions, with a final realisation that Spirit and Matter are one and indivisible. Trump XXI is said to be the celebration of the accomplishment of the Great Work, the Seventh Initiation, when Cosmic rebirth completes the process of involution in Malkuth, the Fifth Initiation which takes place in the heart

of the Seeker. The Seventh Initiation in the esoteric sense is verily
Full Attainment or Adeptship, the quintessence of Jivanmukti,
but is this finality? The mystic has become the Adept, can he now
face yet another higher initiation and become a God? This in all
seriousness is not fantastic speculation, for it is the privilege of the
individual Seeker to TRY.

> "For what contend the wise? for nothing less
> Than that the soul, freed from the bond of sense,
> And to her God restored by evidence
> Of things not seen, drawn forth from their recess,
> Root there, and not in forms, her holiness."

(Wordsworth)

MINOR ARCANA

KING OF PENTACLES

KING OF WANDS

KINGS

KING OF CUPS

KING OF SWORDS

MINOR ARCANA

QUEEN OF PENTACLES

QUEEN OF WANDS

QUEENS

QUEEN OF CUPS

QUEEN OF SWORDS

MINOR ARCANA

HORSEMAN OF PENTACLES

HORSEMAN OF WANDS

HORSEMEN

HORSEMAN OF CUPS

HORSEMAN OF SWORDS

MINOR ARCANA

PAGE OF PENTACLES

PAGES

PAGE OF WANDS

PAGE OF CUPS

PAGE OF SWORDS

MINOR ARCANA

ACE OF PENTACLES

ACES

ACE OF WANDS

ACE OF CUPS

ACE OF SWORDS

CHAPTER XXIII

SOME DIVINATORY ASPECTS OF THE
SIXTEEN COURT CARDS
AND
THE FOUR ACES

It is rather unfortunate that the word "divination" generally has a vulgar connotation linking it with the practice of Black Magic. To set the record straight, Divination is the spiritual diagnosis of a human problem in order to ascertain the subtle influences which are involved, which knowledge can assist in resolving the problem, or in the last analysis turn what appears to be a hopeless situation or state of affairs to the advantage of the querent.

In the Book of Thoth, or the Book of Hermes, better known as the Tarot, the overall virtues advocated by Hermes Trismegistus, thrice great Hermes, on all three planes of existence, are to dare, to be silent, to know and to will. In the Tarot is contained the complete answer to every question posed by the Earth-traveller, whether it affects the mental, astral, or physical planes. There are conflicting opinions as to where the Tarot originated, but without entering into the polemics of this issue, suffice it to say that we can be reasonably sure that the Tarot had its origin in ancient Egypt, and was as today a loose-leaf book illustrated with symbols on each of its seventy-eight pages. There are quite a few Tarot packs with varying symbology available today, in some of which the imagination of the artist runs riot to the detriment of the arcane value of the symbology. The famous Marseille Tarot is the Tarot pack recommended to the exclusion of all others, for in the Marseille Tarot we have the exact representation of the original symbology of the ancient initiate-priests of the temples of the Nile,

F

even though the characters depicted are wearing costumes which appear to be of the Renaissance period in Europe.

The seventy-eight cards of the Tarot, with particular reference to the twenty-two cards of the Major Arcana or Tarot Trumps, enable the mystic to communicate with his own higher mind, his own Electronic Brain. The mystic's super-consciousness feeds back the answer to a query via the symbology of the Tarot cards, for symbols are the universal language of the soul. The feed-back sheds light on the life of man the Microcosm here and now, and also on the Macrocosm, all the outer worlds and conditions. The fifty-six cards of the Minor Arcana correspond more closely to our pack of modern playing cards. The Tarot Minor Arcana is arranged in four suits of fourteen cards, each suit having four Court cards, a King, a Queen, a Knight, and a Page sometimes referred to as a Knave, and ten plain cards numbered from one to ten. The Ace in each suit ranks as a unit and is not regarded as a Court card.

Suits of the Tarot Minor Arcana	*Modern Playing Cards*
Wands or Sceptres represent the Business world of practical realities, and worldly glory.	Clubs
Cups stand for one's affections, hopes and joys, and for peace and harmony generally.	Hearts
Swords threaten danger ahead, misfortune, suffering, and the cruel cuts of Fate.	Spades
Pentacles refer to money, and fortune generally.	Diamonds

Reversed Cards. A reversed card diminishes its dynamic esoteric and exoteric value when it is a good card. When however a bad card is reversed, its adverse implications are lessened. A male card when reversed may well indicate the female sex, and vice-versa. The reversal of a Court card could, within the frame of its reference, indicate a person of either male or female leanings or temperament. A Court card reversed should always be read in the light of its adjacent cards and in terms of the problem to be resolved.

The Four Kings
or
The Gifts of the Magi

The King of Sceptres/Wands—a dark friendly man. Generally a family man, helpful in successful business ventures. Reversed—the opposite.

The King of Sceptres is the Keeper of the Astral Halls of Records, who will enable the querent to tap the Akashic Records. He is the source of inspiration from whence the conscious mind garners knowledge during sleep; knowledge and help which will not be refused when the querent signals "Mayday".

The King of Cups—a fair friendly man, probably a bachelor. Possibly connected with the Law or the Church. Reversed—the opposite.

The King of Cups assists the querent in attracting the good-will of his fellows, so as to live in peace and harmony.

The King of Swords—A dark man of power, who could be a soldier. Reversed—treacherous and to be distrusted.

On the credit side the King of Swords helps the querent to overcome such evil people whose man object in life is the spread of mischief. Arcane help will also be given in turning adversity to good use to the benefit of the querent.

The King of Pentacles—a fair friendly man, if not reversed. He could also be a miser or a rich man.

"Money does not grow on trees", but the King of Pentacles is the Lord of the Money Tree, who will assist the querent in directing and planting (i.e. applying) the seeds of his own efforts in such a way as to show the most productive results.

The Four Queens
or
The Consorts of the Magi

The Queen of Sceptres/Wands/Rods—a dark friendly, prudent and serious woman, probably a mother and married. Reversed—indicates suspicion, jealousy and mistrust.

Occultwise, the Queen of Sceptres is the "Queen of the Throne of Flame" who carries the flaming ever-lit torch of knowledge. Her specific work is to open up all channels of knowledge to the earnest querent seeking knowledge both mundane and arcane. The mental call for assistance must of necessity be made for there is nothing shameful in not knowing and wanting to know, for the beginning of knowledge is a sense of one's limitations.

The Queens of Cups—a fair friendly woman. Reversed—a mistress, or one who may leave cause for regret.

The Queen of Cups is the "Queen of the Throne of the Waters" all powerful in love affairs.

The Queen of Swords—A dark woman who represents worldly prestige of a negative order in terms of the querent's destiny. Reversed—scandal, gossip, loneliness, and unhappiness.

The Queen of Swords is the "Queen of the Thrones of the Air" who brings opportunity in proportion to the talent of the querent by the control of the natural forces symbolically represented by Air.

The Queen of Pentacles—a fair wealthy woman, or a fair woman with the urge to make money. Reversed—difficult financial circumstances.

The Queen of Pentacles is the "Queen of the Thrones of the Earth", who will assist in personal welfare and the fulfilment of material wishes. The human error to be avoided here is greed, for this will necessarily spell occult disaster and failure to the detriment of the querent.

The Four Knights

"I hold it true that thoughts are things
Endowed with being breath and wings;
And that we send them forth to fill
The world with good results or ill."
(Ella Wheeler Wilcox)

To the sincere querent who has endeavoured to understand at least some of the mysteries of the Major Arcana, the four Knights of the Minor Arcana will be seen in their true symbolical perspective. These Chevaliers represent the thoughts of men for whom the Kings stand in a Tarot spread. If in a spread the Knight of Sceptres lies close to the querent's card, then it would be the King of Sceptres, namely, the man actually represented by the Knight, who has the querent in mind or will influence the querent.

Alternatively, any Knight in a spread might represent some phase of the querent's own thought form. Thoughts make magic and true magic is the art of willing and compelling things to happen, and this indeed is the message of the four Chevaliers.

The Knight of Sceptres—a friendly dark, helpful young man of prudent thoughts.

The Knight of Cups—a fair, friendly young man, representing a lover or his thoughts.

The Knight of Swords—a dark treacherous young man or his thoughts. An enemy.

The Knight of Pentacles—a fair young man or his thoughts. A new male friend who is a stranger.

The moral conveyed by the four Chevaliers is that one should endeavour not to have pessimistic thoughts, for these are non-creative thoughts in terms of the future. The prominence of the Sword suit in a spread, would clearly indicate the pessimism and non-creative thoughts of a querent.

The Four Pages

Pages are adolescents of either sex, and are often representative of the thoughts and intentions of others in regard to the querent.

The Page of Sceptres—a dark young person, the bearer of news from relatives. Reversed—Extravagance or thriftlessness as a means of escapism when things seem to go wrong. Alternatively, the Page of Sceptres could represent that part of the mind which is susceptible to impressions, and which gives a warning that something is amiss.

The Page of Cups—a fair young friendly person, representing honesty and faithfulness, a lover of mysticism, or a messenger. Reversed—some obstacle that is hadicapping a love affair.

The Page of Swords—a dark young person bearing evil news: could also stand for a rival. Reversed—the exposure of a false friend. Alternatively, a person of ill-habits who becomes a victim of his own Karma.

The Page of Pentacles—a fair young person, careful and diligent. Reversed—an ignorant yet wealthy person, who could be avaricious and enslaved to money.

The Four Aces

Each of the four Aces of the Minor Arcana has rulership over an element, and represents occult forces with a direct bearing on mankind, subject to the framework of man-made law and government in an ordered society.

The Ace of Sceptres has rulership of the element of fire, with its dominion in the East. It represents the life-force and in essence the growth processes of all things created. Its keynote is strength, energy and the acceleration of everything nascent in the natural order. It corresponds to the first house of a horoscope, namely, the querent. In a Tarot spread it represents growth and development. When reversed it indicates personal aspects in the life or health of the querent.

The Ace of Cups with rulership over water, is associated with the female aspect of the Planetary Being, and corresponds to the fourth house of a horoscope, namely, home interests and house property. In a Tarot spread it symbolises beauty, happiness and productiveness, and also the satisfactory conclusion of any matter under reference. Reversed, the Ace of Cups represents self-destruction in terms of over-indulgence and waste, with resultant deterioration of the mental and moral fibre of the querent on his self-imposed road to ruin.

The Ace of Swords has dominion over the air, and symbolises forces which can be invoked by the human will. It connects with the seventh house of a horoscope, namely, with partners in business or marriage, and with human associations generally. When upright the Ace of Swords is Excalibur the sword of righteousness invoking divine spirituality on the querent. When the sword point is reversed, destructive forces are invoked warning the querent against enemies. Ritual swords are still used on occasions during ceremonial magic.

The Ace of Pentacles has dominion over the earth in all its mundane affairs. It links with the tenth house in a horoscope, namely, occupation, status, ambitions, relationship with authorities, wealth and power. In a Tarot spread this Ace is an omen of success in connexion with business, status and ambitions. When reversed, it is a warning to the querent that he is pursuing the shadow for the unattainable substance.

CHAPTER XXIV

THE TAROT MASTER PLAN
LEADING TO
SOME FURTHER DIVINATORY ASPECTS

The twenty-two Trumps of the Major Arcana symbolise man's whole initiatory journey whilst passing through the processes of Involution and Evolution. The first ten Trumps are a description of Involution, whilst the remaining twelve Trumps describe the successive phases of Evolution on the road to complete Adeptship. Arcanum XIII—The Reaper, signifying both Death and Resurrection, represents a pivotal point of absolute inertia where Involution stops and Evolution commences with Arcanum XIV—Temperance or the Angel of Time.

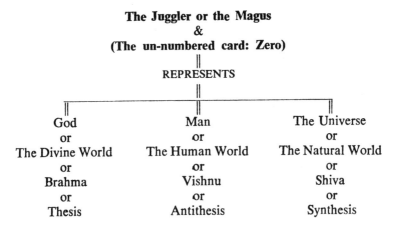

The Juggler or the Magus
&
(The un-numbered card: Zero)
‖
REPRESENTS
‖

‖	‖	‖
God	Man	The Universe
or	or	or
The Divine World	The Human World	The Natural World
or	or	or
Brahma	Vishnu	Shiva
or	or	or
Thesis	Antithesis	Synthesis

The Magus controls the three mystic divisions of the Tarot Major Arcana, for he is the triune aspect of God, man, and the Universe. The Tarot Trumps from Arcana I to XXI fall into the self-same pattern of God, Man and the Universe, forming three* septenaries or groups of seven, tracing the spiritual ascent of man seeking the Spark Divine. Proceeding through Involution and Evolution, shedding his Karmas through successive incarnations, the Magus finally stands before the throne of God. Earth-wise, the juggler or the Magus, the uncertain initiate, the erstwhile Fool, the un-numbered card, having taken the first step has now by reason of his diligence and awareness become the accomplished Mage. The un-numbered Fool is raised to pristine glory in Trump XXI—"The World".

The Three Septenary divisions of the Major Arcana

The 1st Septenary

The creation of the Magus through the process of Involution, whereby the Mental Power of Man assisted by his intellect, dominates his development.

	Arcanum	*Signification key*
I	The Magus	Will
II	Isis	Wisdom
III	The Empress	Action
IV	The Emperor	Realisation
V	The Great Hierophant	Mercy
VI	The Lovers	Harmony
VII	The Chariot	Triumph

---

* c.f. *The three septenaries of the Apocalypse*
1. Seven seals to open, meaning seven mysteries to be learned and seven difficulties to be overcome.
2. Seven trumpets to sound, being seven utterances to understand.
3. Seven vials to empty, which signify seven substances which must be volatilised and fixed.   (Eliphas Levi)

The 2nd Septenary

The spiritual trials of the Magus, beset by Involution and Evolution, with an evolutionary turning point at Arcanum XI—"Strength", assisted by the Solar Power of the Gnostic Lion, as a result of which, the moral side of the Seeker is developed particularly in his attitude towards his fellow-men.

	Arcanum	Signification key
VIII	Justice	Justice
IX	The Hermit	Prudence
X	The Wheel of Fortune	Fortune
XI	Strength	Spiritual strength
XII	The Hanged Man	Sacrifice
XIII	The Reaper or Death	Change
XIV	Temperance	Combination

The 3rd Septenary

The spiritual ascent of the Magus to the crest of Evolution, and finally to triumph and Adeptship, relative to the various events of his material life.

	Arcanum	Signification key
XV	The Devil	Fate
XVI	The Struck Tower	Ruin
XVII	The Star	Hope
XVIII	The Moon	Danger
XIX	The Sun	Material Happiness
XX	Judgement	Result
XXI	The World	Completion or Fulfilment

The ten numerical/non-pictorial cards of the Minor Arcana

The ten numerical cards of any suit (Sceptres, Cups, Swords, or Pentacles) have an assisting or detracting value, ranging from the Ace (Unity) to the ten of the suit, dependent on the overall signification of the particular suit under interpretation.

To Recapitulate:

The Four suits of the Minor Arcana	*General signification*
Sceptres or Wands	represents the Business world of practical realities, and also worldly glory.
Cups	stand for one's affections, hopes and joys, and for peace and harmony generally.
Swords	threaten danger ahead, misfortune, suffering, and the cruel cuts of Fate.
Pentacles	refer to money, and to fortune generally.

So far, an attempt has been made to give both the esoteric and exoteric interpretation of the twenty-two Tarot Trumps, the sixteen Court Cards and the four Aces within the limitations of this writer who lays no claim to infallibility, for a detailed assessment of both the Major and Minor Arcana would entail a lifetime of work on the subject which would still leave many questions unanswered. This then is the challenge for the individual Seeker or Querent who will in his own way strive to read the Tarot.

Bearing in mind the general signification of each of the four suits of the Minor Arcana, namely, Sceptres, Cups, Swords, and Pentacles, we may establish that each of the numerical cards ranging from the Ace to the ten of a suit may be interpreted in the light of their particular suit of reference by the following broad meanings attached to each of the cards.

	Numerical Cards of the Minor Arcana	Signification
THESIS		
	Aces	Commencement, news.
	Twos	Letters, journeys, work.
	Threes	Associations, or partnerships
ANTITHESIS		
	Fours	Gains.
	Fives	God, luck.
	Sixes	Social benefits.
SYNTHESIS		
	Sevens	Changes, flux.
	Eights	Expenditure entailing loss.
	Nines	Promising outlooks.
	Tens	Monetary gains.

Paradoxically, all of these significations are likely to be adversely interpreted in the Swords suit, bearing in mind that in any Tarot spread a card should always be interpreted in the light of its adjacent cards and in correlation with the question to be resolved.

The question of TIME

I do not know of any direct method by means of which the Tarot cards can be manipulated and read so as to correctly determine the Time factor with spot-on accuracy. However, this can generally be gauged with fair accuracy by the juxtaposition of cards read in correlation with the particular problem to be resolved.

The Court cards are most helpful in this connexion, for the correspondence of the Court cards with the signs of the Zodiac and the four Seasons, gives an insight into the time factor. In each suit, the first seasonal month represents the month of activity and creativity; the second month, the inactive and passive month; and the third month, that of equilibration. The Page or Knave of a suit represents the period of transition between seasons.

Court Cards	Zodiacal sign and accepted dates	

SCEPTRES/**SPRING**

King	Aries	21 March to 20 April
Queen	Taurus	21 April to 20 May
Knight	Gemini	21 May to 20 June

CUPS/**SUMMER**

King	Cancer	21 June to 20 July
Queen	Leo	21 July to 21 August
Knight	Virgo	22 August to 22 September

SWORDS/**AUTUMN**

King	Libra	23 September to 22 October
Queen	Scorpio	23 October to 22 November
Knight	Sagittarius	23 November to 20 December

PENTACLES/**WINTER**

King	Capricorn	21 December to 19 January
Queen	Aquarius	20 January to 18 February
Knight	Pisces	19 February to 20 March

Reversed Cards See Chapter XXIII

Some Tarot spreads

Whether the Major Arcana* is used separately, or a suit of the Minor Arcana separately, or all seventy-eight cards together; the cards must first be shuffled well by the querent who must concentrate on the problem/s to be resolved. The cards must also be cut by the querent by the right hand if right-handed or alternatively by the left hand.

I think there is a positive value in each Tarot cartomancer employing fewer spreads which suit his particular psyche, than in dabbling in many spreads, which might be the road to confusion and inaccuracy.

Three spreads are only indicated (as used by the writer) here, but doubtlessly anyone sufficiently interested in the subject could devise many more which may well be highly successful.

* NOTE ON THE MAJOR ARCANA OR TAROT TRUMPS

The expert Tarot delineator can obtain equally accurate results using ordinary playing cards in lieu of the Tarot Trumps, as indicated below. The playing cards should be marked at the top with a pencil cross to indicate their upright positions, in order that reversed cards might be interpreted correctly. However, this method is not advocated for the dilettante, for it is only the expert thoroughly conversant with the mnemonic impact of the Tarot symbology who is in a position to read the Magian secrets contained therein and correlate them with the issues to be resolved.

Arcanum	Tarot Trump	Ordinary Playing Card
Zero	The Fool	The Joker
I	The Juggler	King of Diamonds
II	The High Priestess	Queen of Diamonds
III	The Empress	Queen of Clubs
IV	The Emperor	King of Clubs
V	The Great Hierophant	Knave of Hearts
VI	The Lovers	Queen of Hearts
VII	The Chariot	Nine of Hearts
VIII	The Balance	King of Hearts
IX	The Hermit	Knave of Clubs
X	The Wheel of Fortune	Nine of Diamonds
XI	The Enchantress	Nine of Clubs
XII	The Hanged Man	Knave of Diamonds
XIII	The Reaper	Ace of Spades
XIV	Temperance	Ace of Clubs
XV	The Devil	Knave of Spades
XVI	The Struck Tower	Nine of Spades
XVII	The Star	Ace of Diamonds
XVIII	The Moon	King of Spades
XIX	The Sun	Ace of Hearts
XX	The Last Judgement	Queen of Spades
XXI	The World	Ten of Hearts

Quick Decision Spreads

The Star spread based on the upright pentagram

It might be advisable to have a large piece of thick cardboard or a piece of three-ply wood on which an upright pentagram is drawn.

After the querent has shuffled and cut the cards, the Tarot delineator deals them face upwards clockwise round the Star starting at the apex, with the sixth card placed in the centre of the Star. This sixth card represents the querent and is in fact the control card. The card at the apex of the star has the closest affinity with the control card, the card in position two the next nearest affinity and so on till card five which has the least affinity with the centre card. The cards must be read off commencing with the card in position one. When a question of time is involved, the card in position one is the nearest in time, and the card in position five the furtherest off in terms of time. Either the whole Tarot pack may be used or only the Major Arcana.

The spread of Six using only the Major Arcana

After the querent has shuffled and cut the cards, the Tarot reader deals them face upwards in two rows of three cards each, starting in each case from left to right, thus:

1	2	3
4	5	6

The central cards in each of the lines, namely, the cards in positions two and five, are the control cards and determine the final result of the analysis. On the time scale the events indicated by the cards in positions 1, 2, and 3, precede such events as may be indicated by the cards in the second line in positions 4, 5, and 6.

The Horoscope spread

In the Horoscope spread, the whole Tarot pack (or the Major Arcana only) is shuffled and cut by the querent as before. The

Tarot delineator then deals out twelve cards in a circle as in the accompanying figure, commencing from number one, anti-clock-wise, with a thirteenth card in the centre which serves as a control card for this spread and represents the querent. The twelve cards when in position, are each said to represent the twelve divisions or Houses of a Horoscope as in the allied art of Astrology. Each of the cards should be interpreted in correlation with its placement in its respective House.

A brief list of the activities and/or people, proper to each Solar House is as follows:

Solar House		Activities/People
1	.....	Represents the querent.
2	.....	his money and his movable possessions.
3	.....	his brothers and sisters, his mental outlook, short journeys, changes, letters, and telephone calls.
4	.....	his home and family, his property and immovable possessions.
5	.....	his children, particularly his first child; sport, pleasure and speculation.
6	.....	Health, people of inferior position, and conditions of service.
7	.....	Matrimony, courtships, work associates, general relations with other people.
8	.....	Money belonging to others, insurances, taxation.
9	.....	Future arrangements, lengthy travel, legal questions, relaxations.
10	.....	Career and status, ambitions, relationships with authorities.

11   .....   Friendships, hopes, wishes, clubs and societies, creature comforts.

12   .....   Secret enemies, the results of past activities, prisons and hospitals. The hidden reservations in the querent's mind about the question/s to be answered.

The State of the Nation

The basic method used for a querent's personal horoscope using the Tarot horoscope spread, may also be used in assessing the destiny of a country for the ensuing twelve months. The thirteenth card in the centre of the layout will necessarily represent the country or nation, and will, as before, be the control card. Brief significations for each of the Solar Houses with special reference to Britain, are as follows:

Solar House   *Significations*

1   .....   General state of the nation.

2   .....   Trade, finances, revenue, banks, Stock Exchange, money values.

3   .....   Newspapers, telephones, railways, traffic, education, books.

4   .....   Farming, mines, the opposition party.

5   .....   Birth rate, sport, amusements, public morality.

6   .....   Public health, Civil Service, Armed Forces, the working classes.

7   .....   Foreign trade, international relationships, war questions.

8   .....   Financial agreements with other countries, Death rate, the Privy Council.

9   .....   Overseas trade, Churches, Law courts, science, religion.

10   .....   The government, national status, Royalty.

11   .....   Legislature, Parliament, the Lower House, International alliances.

12   .....   Institutions, Hospitals, Prisons.

The occasion may well arise, when the Tarot delineator has to operate without the bodily presence of the querent, and will therefore have to himself shuffle, cut the cards and deal them out in a spread. This ought to offer little difficulty if before the spread is laid and the cards are shuffled and cut, the written query even if contained in a sealed envelope, is held to the forehead at a point between the two eyebrows, and the query or the contents of the sealed envelope be concentrated upon for about thirty seconds.

With continued divinatory practice with both the Major Arcana and the complete Tarot pack of seventy-eight cards, surprising as it may seem, powers of clairvoyance will be developed. Quite often the delineator will assign a meaning to a card which does not reconcile with the accepted views of Tarot authorities. This must be accepted, for the skilled Tarot delineator relies in a great measure on his powers of intuition assisted by the Tarot cards.

APPENDIX I

KARMA

The law governing rebirth is the law of Karma. The word "Karma" literally means "action". According to the Vedanta philosophers, reward and punishment are subject to the law of action and reaction, to wit, the reaction of our own actions. God does not punish the wicked or reward the virtuous. Karma is the manifestation of God's power in the moral order of the world. Man is subject to the law of personal responsibility or Karma. Divine justice or Karma is not cause and effect, for the law of causation is not universal, and is limited in scope. We have to regain our perspective and accept a totally new scale of values, for deviation from the "Golden Mean" of Cleobolus of Lindus, namely Karma, brings into operation the effects of Karma. Thus the maxim of Heraclitus of Ephesus rings true that, "Character is destiny". The commonest of all punishments is ill-health, for imbalance of Spirit creates imbalance of body, a wrong chemical balance conducive to disease. Karma is an impersonal automatic neuter law, the very pivot on which all life turns. Human hopes must not therefore center on the working of an inexorable and blind Karma, but humanity must take a sound moral stand reaching beyond the principle of Karma and yet within it, by being conscious of our responsibilities and fearless of consequences. Then shall Karma stand unveiled, for we shall be conscious of the whole truth, recognising Karma as but two aspects of one Eternal Truth, the Absolute or Brahman.

Since empirical facts and science support the validity of the law of natural causation, similar treatment and scientific research might with fruitful results be applied to the law of Karma for its validation. The late Atom scientist Dr. J. Robert Oppenheimer in the B.B.C. Reith Lectures (1953) speaking on "Uncommon Sense", said that the "indeterminacy" of the atom did not provide a physical basis for free-will. Without questioning the correctness of Dr. Oppenheimer's statement, we must admit that he was thinking ahead of his time, and was therefore whether right or wrong, sure to be misunderstood. In the light of this, a most promising field of investigation with respect to Karma, lies ahead for any investigator with common sense, who would in all probability amaze the world with the uncommon sense of his findings. The law of Karma does not in any way deny a man free-will, for if a man's present condition is determined by his past conduct, his future may in like measure be determined by his present efforts. A man therefore has the freedom to act in any way he pleases, in order that he might so achieve his objectives. It is absurd, therefore, to equate Karma with either Fate or Destiny, for Karma is a stern moral law which cannot be flouted. If Karmic promptings along the paths of virtue did not operate, man would invariably on the stage of world-appearance be attracted equally in two opposite directions, and be unable to make up his mind. Man would thus be a first cousin to the Ass about whom the Greek Sophist Buridan spoke when he said—"If a hungry ass were placed exactly between two haystacks in every respect equal, it would starve to death because there would be no motive why it should go to one rather than to the other." To quote the late Count Louis Hamon—"Time weaves Destiny into Design until in the end Perfection shines through the warp and weft and the God-thought underlying all becomes manifest."

The explanation of the world by the law of Karma alone, would be rationally unsatisfying if we omitted the belief in a supreme power. The law of Karma expresses the moral nature of God, in as much as it makes for righteousness. Salvation is conditional in so far as we make or mar our actions on the earth plane. When we sin therefore, it is not unreasonable to assume that God's forgiveness follows according to our degree of repentance and purification. Hence both sin and salvation, which are made operative by different kinds of actions for which we are alone responsible, are governed by the law of Karma.

APPENDIX II

THE DOCTRINE OF MAYA
Apparent contradictions in the Upanisads

The Upanisads (700-650 B.C.) for all their wealth of esoteric wisdom appear to contradict one another in certain sections as to the reality of the world when correlated with Brahman. Sankara* makes short work of these apparent contradictions by his doctrine

* SANKARA.

Sankara or Sankaracharya (Sankara + acharya = Auspicious + spiritual teacher or guide)—788-820 A.D., was a great religious reformer and teacher of the Vedanta philosophy who was born in the Malabar district in the Deccan massif of India. Turning ascetic in his eighth year, he became the disciple of Govinda, a famous hermit who then lived in a mountain cell on the banks of the Nerbudda river. Sankara is said to have written his commentary on the Brahma-sutra in his twelfth year. Later he wrote commentaries on ten Upanisads.

Sankara's main thesis is to show the identity between Brahman (God) and Atman (the Self); and that Brahman alone is the Ultimate Reality, for all else is Maya (illusion). He held that we must worship a First Cause in our own way, but without any comprehension of reality, for all the reality of the world is contained in God in the form of reality. What Sankara possibly overlooked is that God also contains the world as an idea in His intellect. The god Siva was Sankara's special object of worship, and he is believed to have been the incarnation of Siva. Sankara died at Kedarnath in the Himalayas at the early age of thirty-two.

of Maya which postulates the ultimate falsity of the world. The world being an effect is unreal; the cause only is real, and that cause is Brahman. The implication is that the world has no independent reality, not that it is false. The multiple manifestations of Brahman on the world-stage constitute as many sense-objects, and this is why Atman or Supreme Self appears as manifold. Brahman is homogenous, without cause or effect, and is synonymous with Atman, "the inner self that sees, hears, thinks, understands, knows; the perceiver of everything. This is the teaching of all Vendanta texts—the gist of them. It leads to immortality and fearlessness." (Sankara's commentary on the Brihadaranyka Upanisad.)

Sense-objects, according to Sankara, have grades of reality. Such differences however are not real in the ultimate sense, for Brahman or Atman alone are real. Though difference depends upon unity; unity does not depend upon difference, for unity exists per se. Owing to lack of right knowledge a piece of rope might at first glance be mistaken for a snake—therefore knowledge of an object does not require its real existence, for the truth when known removes ignorance. "Brahman is not the author of ignorance nor subject to error", says Sankara.

Sankara and Maya

Maya is "that which is not", or illusory appearance. However, Maya is not false knowledge, for the latter is an attribute of the Self, and an attribute cannot have another attribute. Knowledge destroys Maya at its foundations. With the destruction of Maya by the knowledge of Brahman, nothing remains but the Self. "It is ignorance that conjures up the idea of the non-self; strictly speaking there is nothing but the Self. Therefore when one truly realises the unity of the Self, there cannot be any consciousness of actions, their factors and their results." (Sankara's commentary on the Brihadaranyaka Upanisad.) Whilst ignorance is relative existence consisting of name, form and actions; the Inner Self is the seat of knowledge.

The principle of Maya makes world and soul appear as Divine participations existing outside GOD. However, Divine participability is an illusion for participability in God is impossible.

Sankara admits of the validity of morality and religion, but only
within the fabric of Maya, the Dream. To the mystic remains the
task of transcending his absolute self-realisation. The purpose of
Maya is a negative approach to the revelation of God. The dream
almost loses its hold on the soul when the soul performs its lawful
activities without any self-interest. Rising ever upwards the soul
after a protracted and lengthy struggle at last sheds its worldly
and bodily attachment, till finally Cosmic Consciousness is experi-
enced, and at the moment of death, the soul and God become ONE.

In Maya we impose the plane of externality and finitude on
God. Maya when associated with God, the Principle of Reality,
becomes the principle of externality in God, enabling Him to
receive the world within Himself. Hence Maya makes God omni-
potent, omniscient and omnipresent, turning Him into the Creator,
Preserver and Destroyer of the world. To God Maya adds the
passive possibility of the world—the active possibility of the world
is inherent in Him. Maya explains, therefore, only an apparent
and illusory creation, rendering God apt to appear and not to
exist in the world-form. Maya is the principle which deforms
God, the soul and nature at the same time, for Maya is a conceived form that is in God and yet cannot be in God, to wit, a
deformity. Maya is thus the cause for the huge blunders of the
soul.

Mistaking the shadow for the substance, the piece of rope for
a snake, in our state of self-delusion, are examples of Sankara's
analysis of Avidya (erroneous perception or false knowledge). "The
error of judgement is due to the element of interpretation or what
our thought superimposes on the ground." (S. Radhakrishnan.)
Avidya is but our finite consciousness, our finitude, and can be
checked in its course. The double destiny of Maya is first, to hide
God in a veil of externality away from Nature and the soul; and
secondly, to hide Nature away from the soul and vice versa. The
purpose of Maya, the principle of illusion, is to make possible
a wholesale reduction of souls and Nature to God, for God contains in His Absoluteness both the world and souls.

Sankara's world is an illusion in so far as it exists outside
or inside God, as an aspect of Him. However, since there is
but one Absolute Reality which contains the real world of relative
reality in the form of Reality, one cannot rationally consider the
world as an unreality. There is no illusion in a world existing

THE TAROT OF THE MAGI

outside God as a reproduction of God, since such a world comes
from Reality and is real *by* and *for* this Reality. Sankara's world
is therefore not an illusion. "Illusion always rests upon illusion;
it never rests upon God. the Truth, the Atman. You are never in
illusion; it is illusion that is in you, before you." (Swami Vive-
kananda.)

The selfish man, however, lives in the world according to his
own dictates without referring himself at all to God. Such a world
system existing only in the mind of a selfish man would be an
illusion—Maya. Sankara explains the origin and diversity of the
world of mind and matter by resorting to the principle of Maya.
According to him, every empirical action is true, so long as true
knowledge of the Atman is not attained. On the practical side
Sankara indicates that contemplation must follow asceticism in
order that we may become God-centred, surrendering ourselves
to Him on a basis of quid pro quo. Although this concept is
framed in mythological language, we should note that Krishna is
also Brahma the Absolute, and Bhagavan the personal God.

There is no association of Brahma with Maya, for how can
reality associate with the illusory? The falsehood of the world-
appearance belongs to an indefinite category which is neither "sat"
(is) nor "asat" (is not) in any absolute sense. Brahma the Supreme
Being, the Reality, is "Sat". The right comprehension of reality
will prove beyond doubt that the world never did, does not, and
will never exist again, to wit, "is not". As much false as the
world-appearance itself, is the denial of the world-appearance.
With right knowledge comes the sublime truth that Brahma or
Self alone is reality, is true, and that not only is positive world-
appearance false, but false also is the falsehood itself. Sankara
leaves God untouched in His plane of Absolute Simplicity, explain-
ing the world in terms of immanent creation, maintaining at the
same time God's transcendency. God is not the material cause of
the world. It is the world which brings contradiction within reality.
Therefore, God alone is Real, and the world is not. Sankara
presupposes that there is no inward passivity of God, for He is
the substratum and the world is His form. However, to explain
the world from outside God is impossible unless one utilises the
idea of unreality and illusion, namely, Maya.

The principle of Maya makes us see one and the same Reality
distributed into three reals—God, the Soul and Nature—external

to one another, yet correlated. The world following its own laws of unreality, appears as real within itself, for it has its own apparent or dream reality. The soul considered outside God is Maya, for outside God the soul is real by Absolute Reality. When looking inwards the soul looks itself away into God. In the world, however, the inner look vanishes, and the soul looks away from God and itself into Nature. Since Nature has no visibility by itself, the soul lends Nature its own light and therefore its own self. The light of the soul which is itself, illumines Nature, with which it identifies itself. Krishna makes clear the identification of the soul with the coarse body when he tells Arjuna: "For to the born sure is death, to the dead sure is birth, so for an issue that may not be escaped thou dost not well to sorrow." (Bhagavadgita.) The coarse body only is affected by the import of Krishna's words: "As the body's tenant goes through childhood and manhood and old age in this body, so does it pass to other bodies; the wise man is not confounded therein." (Bhagavadgita.) The coarse body only migrates from object to object in order to learn the lesson that all objects are but different aspects of one reality. "When he perceives that several existences of born beings abide in one, and thence traces their manifoldness, then he wins to Brahma." (Bhagavadgita.) Externally, the soul is selfness itself, and cannot be identified with the appearance of gross matter: such is Maya.

It is an illusion to say that the soul wanders from body to body according to its deserts, for it is the subtle bdoy that transmigrates and not the soul. The subtle body dissolves at liberation. The soul sees the material world and comes into contact with material objects, through the subtle and coarse body. The soul takes into itself the faculties of nurture when it identifies itself with the living material of the world. Nature helped by the awareness of the soul makes us conscious of pain and pleasure. However, in reality the impressions of pain and pleasure are operations of Nature. The world is powerless over us when we abandon the plane of the senses. The unfettered soul can only realise ONENESS when it identifies itself with God the Absolute Light. The soul whilst identifying itself with the principle of individuality is not imprisoned within such narrow limitations. Material Nature merely gives the soul a limited abode of utter exteriority. The soul is self-deluded and self-alienated in so far as its relationship exists with Nature.

Criticism of Sankara's Maya

Man's goal is Moksa or liberation. Since Sankara does not directly equate Moksa with Karma, it is often said that he fosters inaction, attaching no importance to Karma. Such opinions are far removed from the truth, for though Karma causes bondage, Man is the arbiter of his own fate, for his life is shaped by Karmas done in previous births, whose fruits he reaps. We do not suffer for the sins of others, nor are we redeemed by the vicarious atonement of Jesus. What we are, and what we shall be are autonomously determined by our own Karmas, which shape our future careers. In order to progress on the earthly plane, man must with the aid of his Free Will rise ever upward spiritually, using morality as a stepping-stone and not as a stopping place, as Dr. Radhakrishnan has very aptly put the issue. The Jivanmukti who has acquired Moksa here and now, must not be judged from a fallible worldly standpoint, for he is indeed a king amongst men, an Adept, who though unfettered by moral laws, works unstintingly for the commonweal. Cosmic Consciousness is his, to have and to hold for ever and a day.

"When all the ties of the heart are severed here on earth,
    then the mortal becomes immortal—here ends the teaching."

(Katha Upanisad)

APPENDIX III

TABLE SHOWING THE CORRESPONDENCE BETWEEN THE MAJOR ARCANA AND THE HEBREW ALPHABET

No.	Major Arcana	Hebrew Alphabet	Corresponding letter	Numerical power	General Exoteric Signification
0	The Fool	Aleph	—	1	Unity, the Astral Light
1	The Magician	Beth	B	2	Being, mind, man, or God
2	The High Priestess	Gimel	G	3	Isis and her veiled mysteries
3	The Empress	Daleth	D	4	The Woman clothed with the Sun
4	The Emperor	He	H	5	Will-power. Initiation.
5	The Great Hierophant	Vau	W	6	Divine instruction
6	The Lovers	Zain	Z	7	Antagonism, combination, equilibrium
7	The Chariot	Cheth	C	8	Triumph, royalty, priesthood
8	The Balance	Teth	T	9	Justice

#	Card	Hebrew	Letter	Value	Meaning
9	The Hermit	Yod	Y	10	Prudence
10	The Wheel of Fortune	Kaph	C	20	Destiny, fortune
11	The Enchantress	Lamed	L	30	Fortitude, trials surmounted
12	The Hanged Man	Mem	M	40	Sacrifice
13	The Reaper	Nun	N	50	Death, change.
14	Temperance	Samech	S	60	Temperance, economy
15	The Devil	Ayin	—	70	Immense force or power for good or evil
16	The Lightning-struck Tower	Peh	P	80	Ruin, deception
17	The Star	Tzaddi	TZ	90	Hope
18	The Moon	Koph	K	100	Hidden enemies, danger
19	The Sun	Resh	R	200	Change of position
20	The Last Judgement	Shin	SH	300	The Result. Karma
21	The World	Tau	T	400	Assured success

BIBLIOGRAPHY

The Living World of Philosophy. Henry Thomas, Ph.D.
The Meaning of Evolution. George Gaylord Simpson.
Biography of the Earth. George Gamow.
The Bhagavadgita.
The Holy Bible.
The Koran.
Sankara's commentary on the Brihadaranyaka Upanisad.
A history of Indian Philosophy. Vols. I & II. Surendranath Dasgupta, M.A., Ph.D.
Indian Philosophy. Vol. II. S. Radhakrishnan.
Hindu Mysticism according to the Upanisads. Mahendranath Sircar.
How to understand the Tarot. Frank Lind.
How to read the Tarot. Frank Lind.
The Tarot of the Bohemians. Papus.
The Tarot. Paul Foster Case.
The Tarot for Today. Mayananda.
The Tarot. Mouni Sadhu.
The Quest of the Overself. Paul Brunton.
Cosmic Consciousness. Ali Nomad.
Human Destiny. Lecomte du Nouy.
The Dawn of Magic. Louis Pauwels & Jacques Bergier.
Isis Unveiled. H. P. Blavatsky.
The Secret Doctrine. H. P. Blavatsky.
The Secret Doctrine. (The disputed Vol III of 1897). H. P. Blavatsky.
The Legend of the Wandering Jew. Joseph Gaer.
Amulets and Talismans. Sir E. A. Wallis Budge, K.T.
The History of Magic. Kurt Seligmann.
Transcendental Magic. Eliphas Levi.
The History of Magic. Eliphas Levi.
Flying Saucers through the Ages. Paul Thomas.
Anatomy of a Phenomenon. Jacques Valee.

LIKELY STOCKISTS OF TAROT CARDS

L. N. Fowler & Co. Ltd., 15 New Bridge Street, London, E.C.4.
Hamleys, Regent Street, London, W.1.
Helios Book Service Ltd., 8 The Square, Toddington, Nr. Cheltenham, Gloucestershire.
The Insight Institute, Manor House, Worcester Park, Surrey.
Psychic News Bookshop, 23 Gt. Queen Street, London, W.C.2.
John Waddington Ltd., Wakefield Road, Leeds 10.
Messrs. John M. Watkins, 21 Cecil Court, London, W.C.2.

TAROT PACKS RECOMMENDED

1st Choice—The Marseille pack.
2nd Choice—The Insight Institute pack.
3rd Choice—Waite's pack.